MW01515521

IF ONLY I HAD KNOWN ...

For Katherine O'hara
in friendship over many years
and across many miles!
William R. Purcell
9/24/2011

IF ONLY I HAD KNOWN . . .

TRANSFORMATION TESTIMONIES
IN
SOLILOQUY SERMONS
AND
MONOLOGUE MEDITATIONS

William R. Russell

Parson's Porch Books   Cleveland, Tennessee

2010

Parson's Porch Books
11 Holly Trail, NW
Cleveland, Tennessee 37311

If Only I Had Known . . . by William R. Russell

© 2010 William R. Russell. All rights reserved.
Published 2010.
Printed in the United States of America.

ISBN 978-0-9829413-1-7

No part of this book may be reproduced or transmitted in any form
or by any means, electronic or mechanical, including photocopying,
recording, or by any information storage and retrieval system, without
permission in writing from the publisher.

Unless otherwise noted, all Bible references and quotes are as translated
in THE NEW REVISED STANDARD VERSION BIBLE; copyright
1989, by the Division of Christian Education of the National Council
of the Churches of Christ in the United States of America; published
by Thomas Nelson, Inc., Nashville, Tennessee.

To order additional copies of this book, contact:

Parson's Porch Books
1-423-475-7308
www.parsonsporch.com

In memory of

ANN

who loved me then

and in honor of

SHERRI

who loves me now

TABLE OF CONTENTS

Graduating young, eager and wide-eyed from Princeton Theological Seminary in 1964, I received an incredible appointment to serve as Bryant Kirkland's first assistant minister at the historic Fifth Avenue Presbyterian Church in midtown Manhattan. A winsome, effective and gifted preacher, Dr. Kirkland had been installed the year before as successor to the renowned John Sutherland Bonnell, a Canadian expatriate on whose coattails, one of the elders told me later, I had ridden into the job. Dr. Bonnell was still alive and well, and befriended this young fellow Canadian with encouragement, advice and not a few books from his library.

Dr. Kirkland was well on his way to becoming one of America's most admired preachers in the second half of the twentieth century . . . and I had the rare privilege of sitting behind him on that church's lofty pulpit platform Sunday by Sunday and observing how he did it! At the same time, two of my closest friends in ministry were serving as assistant clergy in nearby Manhattan congregations. Through them, I got to know, appreciate and learn from Norman Vincent Peale of the Marble Collegiate Church farther down Fifth Avenue at Twenty-Third Street, and David H. C. Read of the Madison Avenue Presbyterian Church at Seventy-First Street on the Upper East Side.

Among my Fifth Avenue responsibilities was the care and feeding of the guest preachers from across America who filled our pulpit on summer Sundays while Dr. Kirkland was on vacation. Over the years, I entertained—and studied!—among others: Elam Davies, the silver-tongued Welshman from Fourth Presbyterian Church in Chicago; George Docherty, the irascible Scot who succeeded Peter Marshall at the New York Avenue Presbyterian Church in Washington, DC; Edward L. R. Elson, Senate Chaplain after Dr. Marshall and minister of the National Presbyterian Church, also in Washington; Ernest T. Campbell from Ann Arbor, Michigan, who eventually became the preacher at the Riverside Church on Manhattan's Upper West Side; and William Sloan Coffin, the always-controversial Yale University Chaplain.

I hope I am not just "name-dropping!" I honor the memory of the friendship and mentoring of each of these pulpit giants, and I acknowledge their inspiration and influence upon my own understanding of both the theology and the art of preaching.

One troubling observation I made during my early and formative years of ministry was that few, if any, of these and other prominent pulpiteers were ever in their own pulpits on the "low" Sundays after Christmas and Easter. Because, at Fifth Avenue, it was *only* on Sundays like those that I was ever allowed to preach, I recognized that the people scattered in the nearly-empty pews were by and large the true stalwarts of the congregation, the very people who, in my youthful idealism, I felt should be getting the *best* the church had to offer . . . not the *second-* (or, as in my humble status, the *third-*) string substitute.

At first, I confess, I wasn't quite humble enough to suspect

that the reason *why* the attendance was so sparse on those occasions was *because* I was the preacher . . . until one blizzardy
end-of-December Sunday when I heard the whispered encouragement of the Sexton as I was about to enter the sanctuary.
Having "counted the house" through a peep-hole in the door
that led to the pulpit platform, he reassured me: "Never mind,
Mr. Russell; there wouldn't be any more people here even if Dr.
Kirkland or Mr. Jones (the Associate Minister) were preaching!"

It was probably right about then that I first vowed—to God
and to myself—that, if I were ever privileged to preach regularly
from my own pulpit, I would never absent myself from it—and
from the stalwarts seated before it—on the post-Christmas and
post-Easter "low" Sundays of my ministry.

So it was out of that vow that the soliloquy sermons in this
collection first came to be. Webster's dictionaries say that a *soliloquy* is "a speech . . . in which a character, alone or as if alone,
discloses innermost thoughts." That is precisely what the first
two attempts were (see the background commentaries to CHAP-
TERS IV and XV, "If Only I Had Known . . ." and "In the Upper
Room . . . Again." Over the years and decades since, I realize,
my messages have "morphed" into what might more exactly be
termed *monologues*. But that term had, by then, taken on a significance inescapably associated with Johnny Carson, Jay Leno
and David Letterman—with whom I didn't feel I wanted to be
compared!—and so the original appellation has stuck.

"My own pulpit" was provided to me in 1968, through a
call to become the pastor of the Wyoming Presbyterian Church
in Millburn, New Jersey. A "bellwether" congregation situated

almost halfway between Manhattan and Princeton, the
Wyoming Church seemed almost always to find its way to the
forefront of whatever was on the leading edge of ecclesiastical
life in the nineteen-sixties and -seventies. While I was ministering there, liturgical renewal was coming to the fore in Presbyterian circles: we were "into" chancel drama and dance, lectionary
reading and preaching, revival of ancient and traditional worship forms and practices, and experimentation with whatever
was contemporary and inclusive in music, art, and language.
Somehow—from somewhere—I vaguely remember a gift from
Dr. Bonnell of an old book of sermons, of which I confess I have
long since lost track—the idea came to me for a pair of related
soliloquies, one for the Sunday after Christmas, and the other
for the Sunday after Easter, which would be something special
and surprising for the faithful few in worship on those sparsely
attended Sundays.

My first two efforts were greeted with almost unseemly enthusiasm ... and I was encouraged to continue generating "special and surprising" sermons for unlikely and unexpected
occasions throughout the church year. There will always be a
tender spot in my heart of hearts where I cherish my gratitude
to the people of the Wyoming congregation for encouraging
me in an approach to preaching that has been a hallmark of my
ministry for more than four decades now.

Truth be told, my soliloquy sermons (of which there were
by then eight or ten) evoked the same kind of enthusiasm from
the very different constituency of the Church of St. Andrew
and St. Paul, in the heart of Montreal, Quebec, to which I was
called in 1973 for a decade of ministry in "the cathedral church

of Canadian Presbyterianism." Amidst the seething tensions of the rise of Francophone separatism and the election of the *Parti Québecois* in *la belle province*, the congregation of "the A&P" (as it was affectionately, if somewhat irreverently, known across Canada) worshipped in neo-Gothic splendor and St.-Giles-High-Kirk-of-Scotland tradition, supported by one of the finest pipe organs in the province, certifiably the best church choir in Canada, and lighting and sound systems worthy of any concert hall in North America.

With the aiding and abetting of the church's Director of Music, Wayne Riddell (to whom I owe an undying debt of gratitude), and the then sight-and-sound engineer (the late John Bradley), my growing repertoire of soliloquies was embellished with musical introductions and underlays, subtle lighting and stereophonic amplification, all of which combined to encourage me to write and refine most of the rest of this collection of messages.

After a seven-year hiatus in my preaching ministry, during which my late wife, Ann, and I traveled the world in mission support of the United Bible Societies and ultimately retired from the Canadian Bible Society the victims of ill-health, I received an unexpected call in the autumn of 1989 to return to the United States to become the senior pastor of the First Presbyterian Church of Deerfield, Illinois, a north-shore suburb of Chicago. Eventually, I re-introduced my soliloquy sermons into my preaching schedule . . . and, once again, each effort was met with enthusiastic appreciation, and encouragement to create still more first-person insights into familiar (and sometimes not-so-familiar) Bible stories and characters. It was for a large

women's gathering in Deerfield that I essayed my one and only
attempt to soliloquize a woman's point of view—the only one
of my soliloquy presentations ever to evoke a less-than-luke-
warm response—which taught me an important lesson about
my own limitations, and prompted me to try a very different
approach when I re-introduced "Martha" a dozen years later
under very different circumstances (see the backfround com-
mentery to CHAPTER VII, "The Better Part.")

After a decade of ministry in Deerfield, personal and family
health circumstances led me to accept a call to the First Presbyterian Church of Royal Oak, Michigan, an inner suburb of Detroit less than a half-hour's drive from my ailing parents' home
across the Detroit River in Windsor, Ontario. The people of
the Royal Oak congregation were wonderfully supportive as my
health, and that of my wife and both my parents, went into a
spiral that culminated in the deaths of all three, and my own
withdrawal from ministry due to medical disability. It was in
Royal Oak, I think, as my preaching ministry was reaching its
apparent end, that folks began to say, "You ought to put your
soliloquies into a book!" And so I acknowledge their affirming
advice with profound and lasting gratitude.

At one of the lowest points in my ill health, I vowed to God,
and told my family and friends, that, if I were ever restored to
sufficient vigor to enjoy a preaching ministry again, I would become a "rent-a-rev," and make myself available whenever and
wherever a ministry need presented itself to me. That is exactly
what has happened! In retirement, health and happiness restored largely through the providence of God and the coming
into my life of my bride, Sherri, this old "rent-a-rev" preaches,

teaches, counsels, baptizes, marries and buries people where and when God leads. Interim and supply preaching opportunities have prompted me to re-visit the old familiar characters of my soliloquies, and to re-work their messages for occasions on which one or another of them seem appropriate.

In the summer of 2006, the tragic bereavement of the minister and congregation of the First Presbyterian Church in Chatham, Ontario, not far from my beloved Canadian lake house, resulted in my supplying that pulpit for two months, and in re-working yet again some of my soliloquies into a cohesive series of sermons under the theme "Transformation Testimonies." Beginning with the Old Testament prophet Isaiah, and his musings about whether any of his messianic prophecies would ever come to pass, and ending with the Roman centurion Cornelius receiving Simon Peter's first proclamation of the Gospel to the Gentiles at Caesarea, the series included first-person accounts of the full sweep of the nativity, ministry, triumphal entry, passion, death and resurrection of our Lord, complete with seasonal Scripture readings and hymns, all of which had unexpected and profound impact upon worshippers experiencing all of this outside the usual distractions of the Advent/Christmas/Lent/Easter contexts in which they ordinarily occur.

By the time the summer was over, I realized that I had finally found, albeit almost accidentally, the organizing principle around which I could begin to gather all of my soliloquies into what I hope will be a meaningful volume for other preachers who may discover herein something to spark their own imagination and approach to the art and discipline of preaching.

To God be the glory: great things He hath done!

William R. Russell
Destin, Florida
June 30, 2010

ACKNOWLEDGEMENTS

Without the amiable insistence and effective urging of my friend, John Killinger, I might never have undertaken this project. Thank you, John!

Without the ministry vision and mission vitality of my publisher, David Tullock, and his *Parson's Porch*, I might never have had my manuscript accepted for publication. Thank you, David!

Without the editorial erudition and typographical talents of my editor, John Eric Killinger—John's son, how cool is that?—I am sure this volume would never have been as beautifully prepared and presented as I think it is. Thank you, Eric!

Without the enthusiasm and encouragement of my friends in Florida's Emerald Coast Writers, their president, Joyce Holland, and their most prolific published author, Vicki Hinze, I would never have presumed to have any of my sermons published. Thank you, Joyce, Vicki *et alia*!

Without the supportive interest in and steadfast appreciation of these soliloquies and monologues by my congregations in Millburn, New Jersey, Montreal, Quebec, Deerfield, Illinois, Royal Oak, Michigan and Chatham, Ontario, I would not have persevered with the biblical personalities I have plumbed and preached over the past four decades. Thank you, every Presbyterian of you!

Without the gentle encouragement and sometimes not-so-gentle insistence of my wife, I would by no means have "kept my nose to the grindstone," let alone my fingers on the keyboard, to pull all this material together. Thank you, Sherri!

And, without the grace of God, the love of Christ and the inspiration of their Holy Spirit, "I am nothing" (I Cor. 13:2). Thank you, Jesus!

— I —

ISAIAH

BACKGROUND COMMENTARY

W HAT IS "PROPHECY"—or, more specifically,
prophecy in the Old Testament, and even more
particularly, in the Book of Isaiah? As I prepared
for a church year in which I proposed to preach on some of the
Advent and Lenten readings from Isaiah appointed by the
Common Lectionary,[1] it was almost as though the prophet
himself began to insist to my subconscious that I introduce *him*
to my congregation before I undertook to expound upon his vi-
sions, oracles and admonitions.

Beginning from the consensus of many commentators that
the original source of the prophecies of Isaiah was "inside rather
than outside the central institutions of Judah," and that he
"probably had a group around him" (*disciples* [*sic*], Isa 8:16) who
would have been the first to collect and treasure his words,"[2] my
imagination made Isaiah the scion of a decidedly aristocratic,
traditionally priestly and politically powerful family. His call to
a prophetic career "in the year that King Uzziah died" anchored
him historically in the second half of the eighth century BCE
as a young man with easy access to the court of Uzziah and his
successors.

1. For a fuller discussion of the impact of the Common Lectionary on my
soliloquy sermons, see the Background Commentary on Loukas in CHAP-
TER XX.

2. *The New Interpreter's Bible*, VOL. VI, p. 36.

Given the prophet's many tirades against the emptiness and hypocrisy of Judah's religiosity at that time, it was not difficult to imagine the frustrations and inner conflicts Isaiah must have felt as a youth growing up with such mixed expectations about who and what he was to become. His obedient and at once ambivalent response to his overwhelming vision in the Temple described in chapter 6 seemed to me to set the tone for an understanding of his characteristic prophetic mix of judgment and pleading on God's behalf throughout the three decades or more of his public ministry.

His ultimate confrontation with King Hezekiah during the so-called Assyrian crisis of 705-701 BCE end-bracketed Isaiah's prophetic ministry with astonishing results: ". . . whether because Hezekiah paid tribute or the Lord intervened directly as promised by Isaiah, the Assyrians withdrew without taking the city (of Jerusalem)."[3]

Nevertheless, it was the apparent futility of so much of Isaiah's prophetic ministry—reflected in the "doom and gloom" oracles that punctuate chapters 1-39 of the book—that emerged as the main burden of my message. I felt it was important to prepare my listeners for a series of sermons that would reflect my conviction that people then—and still today—have misunderstood and misinterpreted so much of what appears in the Book of Isaiah. Old Testament prophecy is not "fortune-telling"—it never was!—and I wanted my people to approach Isaiah's life's work from the prophet's own understanding that (as Isaiah himself puts it in the sermon) "God has inspired and directed—and used—me to warn my people—and my king—of what will happen if they don't change their ways . . . personally as well as politically."

3. Ibid., p. 37.

For this monologue, I chose not to try to deal with the form-critical issues of Second and Third Isaiah—the prophet's cryptic reference to working on "my memoirs, and the second volume of my collected oracles" in his old age was as far as I felt I could go until I got into the sermon series proper! Since this introductory sermon was scheduled for the last Sunday before the start of the new church year—Christ the King Sunday—I wanted strong references to the Advent prophecies in chapters 7, 9, 11 and 35. I felt the powerful poignancy of the prophet's painful musings: "I wonder whether the Prince of Peace will ever be born? . . . and when? . . . and where? . . . and to whom? I wonder what he will be like . . . and how he will save his people . . . and if they will listen to him more than they have to the likes of me."

I became convinced that *that* was where the whole monologue needed to end . . . and, in fact, as I wrote and re-wrote it, that conclusion formed and re-formed the whole message.

Since then, I have included this sermon as the first in a series of soliloquies and monologues titled "Transformation Testimonies." No matter the time of year in which the series was to be presented, I have abandoned the appointments of the Common Lectionary, and have included in the Order of Service Isaiah 6 as the Old Testament Lesson and Luke 3 as the Gospel Lesson. The choir and congregation have sung such traditional Advent hymns as "O Come, O Come, Emmanuel," "Come, Thou Long-Expected Jesus," and "On Jordan's Bank the Baptist's Cry," whose texts speak with surprising power and promise when heard and sung outside the "holiday season" context in which we have become accustomed to them.

* * * * *

HERE AM I: SEND ME!

Then I heard the voice of the Lord saying,
"Whom shall I send, and who will go for us?"
And I said, "Here am I; send me!"
(ISAIAH 6:8)

It was the year that King Uzziah died. I remember to this day how I was in the Temple . . . with the other novices . . . praying and burning incense for the king's recovery . . . when I had that first great vision.

Uzziah had been a good king . . . and Judah had known almost two generations of peace and prosperity under his reign. His swift, terrible illness had put an end to all that: rival factions had clustered around the several different claimants to the throne—and Uzziah's chosen heir was still a child—so it looked as though the country was in for a period of uncertainty . . . and maybe even violence.

My prayers for the king's recovery were personal as well as political. Although my family was of the tribe of Aaron—and all the men in it were therefore technically priests—my forebears had risen to great wealth and power as counselors to the royal family. My father was Uzziah's First Minister of State—and the prospect of a struggle for the throne meant danger to him and all his relatives. Many in Jerusalem were jealous of our prestige and influence—to say nothing of our palatial houses filled with treasures and our country estates second only to the king's in size and prosperity. Nevertheless, we truly loved our Promised Land, and sought to serve God's Chosen People with what I like to think was pure patriotism.

But we weren't particularly religious. I was training for the priesthood, true, as had all my ancestors . . . though I secretly longed to follow in my father's political footsteps. So much of what went on in the Temple dissatisfied me: it was a beautiful building . . . adorned with rich artistry . . . and filled day and night with the worship of God . . . but a lot of it seemed empty and meaningless to me.

I could never feel sure that God really wanted all that chanting and wailing and burning and incense and blood and ritual. If I were God, I used to think, I'd rather have people pray to me quietly, and study my Law in the Torah, and meditate upon its real meaning for their everyday lives . . . and then go home and *do* something about it!

It was in the midst of all that that I had the vision that changed my life. I saw God.

Well, I didn't exactly *see* God—I don't think anyone can see God on this side of the grave and live—but I saw and heard and felt things that absolutely convinced me that God was in His

Temple . . . and was confronting me with a claim upon my life from that day on.

It was as though all the customary accoutrements of worship suddenly swelled with meaning and power. The altar became as God's throne . . . and the glory of His being there filled every nook and cranny of the Temple like a velvet train. The golden seraphim suspended above the Ark of the Covenant came alive in adoration and praise . . . and the incense combined with the smoke from the burnt offerings overcame me like a terrifying judgment on all my past selfishness and sinfulness.

I really thought for a moment that I was dying. How could anyone experience God so intensely—and go on living? I blurted out my last confession—probably the first confession I had ever really meant! I felt so unclean . . . so inadequate . . . so ill-equipped to cope with a personal encounter with God.

Then it was as though one of the seraphim ministered to me: the searing heat of God's forgiveness burned through me like a live coal . . . and I felt—not destroyed—but cleansed, purified, forged into sterner stuff. I was, at the same time, humbled and exalted, judged and blessed, set free from my past and enslaved for all eternity.

I heard a voice—thunderous in its stillness—call to me: "Whom shall I send? Who will go for me?" I didn't know where. I didn't know why. I didn't know what for. I only knew that I had to respond: "Here am I: send me!"

A lot has happened since then. If I'd known at the beginning what God had in store for me, I might not have answered so boldly and bravely. But, then, we're not meant to know . . . are we? We're meant to follow . . . and obey . . . and do what we're called to do . . . one day at a time.

For me, God's call meant becoming a prophet, rather than a politician, or even a priest. It meant speaking God's words of judgment and warning and promise to a people who, despite all their religion, are stiff-necked, and hard-hearted, and self-centered. Not that God didn't warn me—right from the start—that mine was to be a thankless—and ultimately a thwarted—ministry . . . trying to tell the truth to men and women whose minds were dulled, whose ears were stopped, whose eyes were shut . . . until they might listen but never comprehend, look but never see, behold but never be healed.

That was probably the worst part of that first vision: the dark side of the defining moment of my life. I cried out "How long, O Lord?" How long must I prophesy in vain? How long must I watch my people slide farther and farther into self-destruction? How long must I wait for my prophecies to find fulfillment?

> *Until cities lie waste without inhabitant, and houses without people, and the land is utterly desolate; until the Lord sends everyone far away, and vast is the emptiness in the midst of the land.*[4]

Now, in my old age, fulfillment appears to be not far off. There used to be many prophets speaking out for God in the Northern Kingdom of Israel, and here in the Southern Kingdom of Judah . . . now only I am left . . . and I've been no more popular, and no more successful, than the rest of them.

I've served under four kings (if you count Uzziah, who died about a month after my vision in the Temple)—and, if anything, the country is in worse shape now than when I began.

---

4. Isaiah 6:11-12.

I've been in disgrace for years—banished from the king's court because Hezekiah no longer wanted to listen to what I had to say. I've been working on my memoirs, and the second volume of my collected oracles—but my career is, in effect, over; my influence is clearly at an end; my impact upon the life and faith of my people seems to have been nil . . . and I still wonder whether any of my prophecies are ever going to come true.

People have misunderstood and misinterpreted almost everything I've ever said. They think that a prophet is like a fortune-teller: grease my palm and I'll tell your future. It isn't like that: it never was! God has inspired and directed—and used—me to warn my people—and my king—of what will happen if they don't change their ways . . . personally as well as politically.

I've tried to tell them that God can't stand their hypocrisy—their paying lip-service to their Creator and then doing whatever they like with their lives. I've tried to show them where their present attitudes and values and policies are leading them, individually and nationally. I've tried to caution them that terrible times are ahead—unless they change their ways—and they will not listen.

They tell me I preach "doom and gloom." They laugh that none of my dire predictions has come to pass. They'd rather put their trust in political alliances than in God's promises. They'd sooner compromise their future than take courage in the present to do what's right . . . and necessary . . . and hard. Even now, they're ready to rely on the empty promises of Rabshakeh, the emissary of the great Sennacherib, King of Assyria, whose armies have overrun most of Judah and are poised to lay siege to Jerusalem itself.[5]

Hezekiah has had a change of heart—prompted more by

5. Isaiah 36:1-37:38.

fear than faith, I suspect—and has sent his servants to me for a new prophecy for these terrible times. I have urged Hezekiah and his courtiers not to be afraid . . . but to pray sincerely to the Lord God for deliverance . . . and apparently they have done so. For the Lord God has just given me an almost unbelievable oracle about Sennacherib:

> *He shall not come into this city, shoot an arrow there, come before it with a shield, or cast up a siege ramp against it. By the way that he came, by the same he shall return; he shall not come into this city* . . .[6]

Now I'm really on the horns of a dilemma . . . not that it matters any more. On the one hand, I fervently pray that this latest word from God proves right . . . and that some of my previous prophecies never do come to pass. I'd rather be proven wrong than have Judah conquered, and Jerusalem destroyed, and the king and his court taken away into captivity—even though I've been absolutely convinced that that's what God intends to let happen unless the people come to their senses. And, even now, I'm not sure that that won't be the eventual outcome of my people's history.[7]

But, on the other hand, a few of my other oracles have been so beautiful . . . so reassuring . . . so full of promise . . . that I'd hate to think they might never come true. I've foreseen—far off, perhaps, but all in God's good time—the birth of a Savior for my people . . . a Prince of Peace whose reign will be one of hope and joy and love. He'll be a Good Shepherd to these silly sheep, and a Wonderful Counselor to those who are frightened, or discouraged, or beaten down. He'll be Emmanuel—"God

---

6. Isaiah 37:33-34.

7. According to Isaiah 37:36-38, Judah was spared defeat at the hands of Sennacherib in 688 BC—only to fall eventually to Nebuchadnezzar, the Babylonian emperor, a century later in 587 BC.

with us"—heaven come to earth in a real person . . . and somehow, I know, he'll make all the difference.[8]

For all the judgment—all the "doom and gloom"—God has had me foretell, I am convinced that God really is a merciful, forgiving, generous Heavenly Father. God doesn't want bad things to happen to His children: that's why God sends prophets like me to every generation to warn people of the consequences of their foolishness and sin.

I wonder where I went wrong in trying to get that message across? I wonder if any of the terrible things I have had to prophesy will come to be? I wonder whether the Prince of Peace will ever be born? . . . and when? . . . and where? . . . and to whom? I wonder what he will be like . . . and how he will save his people . . . and if they will listen to him any more than they have listened to the likes of me.

I wonder . . . I wonder . . .

8. Isaiah 7:14, 9:2-7, 11:1-9.

— II —

CORNELIUS
(PART ONE)

BACKGROUND COMMENTARY

URING MY MINISTRY IN Deerfield, Illinois, I undertook to prepare and present a soliloquy sermon for the Christmas Eve services every *other* year. This was my second effort—for Christmas Eve 1992—to try to re-tell the old familiar story of the Nativity in a fresh and compelling way.

My arrogant young Roman centurion had no name then. His point of view was clearly hostile to the Jews among whom he was living and working—an attitude that was surprisingly prevalent in the North American news media at that time. And his self-centered world-weariness was certainly reflective of the mindset of many of the "yuppies" in my congregation on Chicago's affluent North Shore.

I based the narrative on the Gospel of Luke's Nativity account . . . except for a brief reference to "the light of a particularly brilliant star" which I realize is part of the Gospel of Matthew's tradition of the visit of the Magi.[1] Because I had already used the after-Christmas story of Alphaeus (the innkeeper who refused Joseph and Mary a room in his inn)[2] two years before, I wanted to explore the feelings of guilt and shame provoked by that refusal from another point of view. The centurion's conversation with the innkeeper's daughter evoked a strong link with that previously-told story, and gave the hap-

1. Matthew 2:1ff.
2. See CHAPTER IV, "If Only I Had Known . . ."

less centurion the added burden of having suggested the stable as the venue for the birth of the Messiah.

To add an open-ended poignancy to the end of the soliloquy, I asked the church organist to begin to play the carol melody of "O Little Town of Bethlehem" under my speaking voice during the last paragraph of the message. The choir was primed to begin singing the carol, seated, once I stopped speaking. By the time we got to the second half of the third verse of the carol,

> *No ear may hear His coming,*
> *But in this world of sin,*
> *Where meek souls will receive Him, still*
> *The dear Christ enters in,*

many in each of the three Christmas Eve congregations that year were in tears!

The fourth verse of the carol became not only the centurion's heartfelt prayer, but ours as well, transcending the usual "holiday hoopla" associated with such overly familiar texts:

> *O holy Child of Bethlehem,*
> *Descend to us we pray;*
> *Cast out our sin and enter in,*
> *Be born in us today.*
> *We hear the Christmas angels*
> *The great glad tidings tell;*
> *O come to us, abide with us,*
> *Our Lord Emmanuel!*[3]

As things turned out, I never presented this soliloquy again

---

3. Carol text by Philips Brooks, 1868, as published in *The Presbyterian Hymnal: Hymns, Psalms and Spiritual Songs* (Westminster/John Knox Press, 1990).

until the summer of 2006, when I decided to include it in the
"Transformation Testimonies" series for the First Presbyterian
Church in Chatham, Ontario. As I worked over the ten sermons
I wanted to present in that series, and came to the concluding
messages about Simon Peter's first proclamation of the Gospel
of Jesus Christ to the Gentiles in Caesarea at the home of the
Roman centurion Cornelius—described by Luke as "a devout
man who feared God"[4]—I had a flash of inspiration—or at least
imagination!—that begged me to identify Cornelius and the
beginning of his spiritual quest with that nameless centurion in
Bethlehem thirty-some years before!

I confess that there is absolutely no basis in scripture or tradition for this link. But in the context of the sermon series, it
had a profound impact upon my listeners, and helped them rec-
ognize in "the Christmas story" not just a sweet seasonal scripture reading, but a powerful existential basis for mature and
thoughtful faith.

*   *   *   *   *

---

4. Acts 10:2.

No room

While they were there, the time came
for Mary to deliver her child.
And she gave birth to her firstborn son
and wrapped him in bands of cloth, and laid him in
a manger,
because there was no place for them in the inn.
(LUKE 2:6-7)

My name is Cornelius . . . and I am the youngest centurion ever in the imperial army.

Through the influence of my uncle, Gaius Valerius, a Senator of Rome, I leapfrogged most of the promotion process in the Roman military, and was made commander of my own "century" of a hundred soldiers on my nineteenth birthday. True, I had to accept a posting to the Province of Syria . . . where no one in his right mind wants to go . . . and then endure idle months of ridicule and hostility from Quirinius, the governor, whose family and mine have been at odds for generations: but, to make centurion before the age of twenty, why not?

Eventually, Quirinius, weary of what he called my arrogance, and convinced that I needed to learn some lessons about real life, assigned me to the garrison in Jerusalem—a seething cauldron of intrigue and corruption kept astir by the nominal "king" of the Jews, Herod the Great. Even there, there wasn't much to do militarily: all I learned was how to waste time . . . and squander money . . . and lose my youthful optimism and zest for living.

My first real soldiering began a couple of months ago when I was ordered to provide an armed escort for the head-counters and tax-collectors assigned to register the region of Judea for the first imperial census decreed by Caesar Augustus.[5]

What an unhappy business that is! Every Palestinian male has to travel to his place of birth, with his entire family, to be registered within a period of so many days. The whole country is in an uproar: the highways, such as they are, are crowded with traffic; every inn, in every community we visit, is full to over-flowing; the hardship, the waste, the abuse of power, is truly in-human.

I was already pretty disillusioned by the time we came to Bethlehem . . . a dusty little village with no claim to fame other than that it was the birthplace of one of the first kings of Israel. And that, of course, made everything worse! Every single Jew who claimed descent from the royal lineage of the ancient House of David showed up in Bethlehem in the same two-week period: utter madness!

And what an unhappy, unruly lot they were—so full of what they thought were royal airs and attitudes—so hostile to us Romans, and even more surly toward our Jewish civil ser-vants—so religious, in a weird way, yet so harsh and judgmental and cruel, even to one another. As disenchanted as I was becom-ing with soldiering, and as disturbed as I was feeling about the monumental folly of this census business, Bethlehem finished off any sympathy I might have been harboring for the people

5. Luke 2:1ff.

whose lives had been thrown into chaos by our determination to count and tax them.

Among the things that annoyed me most were the incessant attempts of each day's new arrivals to get accommodation in the only inn around. Had I been willing to rent out my room to the visiting would-be royals, I could have made a small fortune! But it was the one place where I could be sure of some peace and privacy, some rest and relaxation, after the terrible, turbulent workdays I was putting in.

So you can understand that I was utterly unmoved when the innkeeper asked yet again if I would vacate my room for a young couple just arrived from Nazareth, who had neither the means to offer a bribe nor the energy to plead with me on their own behalf.

I remained intransigent, even after the innkeeper's daughter came to me a few hours later, begging the plight of the same couple, whose baby, it appeared, might be born within the next few hours. She persisted. I finally became so exasperated that I yelled at her: "Then move my horse out of the stable, and give them the stall for the night—they're no better than animals, most of them, anyway!"

So, she did: and, that very night, the couple's baby was born . . . under circumstances I can only describe as extraordinary. Just after midnight, whinnying from the paddock awakened me. I got up, pulled my soldier's cloak about my shoulders, and went out to the stable yard to check on my horse—a task made surprisingly easy by the light of a particularly brilliant star.

The lowing of the cattle in the stable caught my attention . . . almost enchanting, it was . . . and got me thinking about

the Galilean couple housed in my horse's stall. Curious, I peeked
in, and was astonished to see that the child had already been
born . . . bathed . . . wrapped in swaddling bands . . . and laid in
the manger. The mother, clearly exhausted, but radiant somehow, rested on her husband's shoulder; both gazed upon their
child with a look that I can only describe as "reverence"; the stable was filled with a sense of peace, of power, of promise, that
made me feel as though I were in the presence of the divine.

It was a disturbing experience. Part of me felt drawn to the
child, wanting to come closer; another part of me felt fearful,
not unwelcome, but unwilling, unsure of how I would be received by the parents my selfishness had sent to the stable with
the animals at such a time as this. Soldier though I be, I
fled . . . and nearly ran into a handful of shepherds hurrying
from a nearby hillside to see what was happening in the stable I
had just left.

All talking at the same time, the shepherds tried to tell me
their story: about an hour before, they had sighted angels visi-
tant in the midnight sky, a heavenly host urging them back to
Bethlehem to adore a new-born king whom they called "Messiah", the long-expected savior of the world foretold by their
prophets of old . . . and who turned out to be, of course, the very
same baby whose birth I had consigned to that stable because I
had refused to give up my bed.

By now, discomfort had given way to dread. What had I
done? Whom had I offended? How could I make amends? I
waited until the shepherds were gone away again, glorifying and
praising their God for all that they have heard and seen tonight
. . . and then I slipped back into the stable, and approached the

family in my horse's stall.

My heart was pounding; my mouth was dry; my palms were sweaty. Nothing in the military had prepared me for a confrontation like this.

The baby's father noticed me first. His eyes widened ... his nostrils flared ... his face clouded with accusation and judgment and sentence all in one. For the first time in my life, really, I saw myself as others must see me: proud, boastful, probably as arrogant as Quirinius said ... spoiled, immature, self-centered ... angry, critical, mean-spirited ... stubborn, hard-hearted, disillusioned ... ambitious, overworked, burned out. I thought: Is that who I am? ... is that what I have become? ... is that how I want to spend the rest of my life?

Before either of us men could say a word, the infant's mother reached up ... touched a silencing finger to her husband's lips ... and spoke to me ... softly ... sweetly ... sincerely:

> This is a night, not for anger, but for peace ...
> not for accusation, but for mercy ...
> not for judgment, but for forgiveness ...
> not for remorse, but for joy ...
> not for despair, but for hope ...
> not for fear, but for love.

> This is a night for the glory of God ...
> and for the redemption of the world ...
> and for the changing of people's lives—
> even your life, centurion.

Then she, too, was silent.

Never has my world been so quiet; never have I felt so alone; never will my life be quite the same. For I glanced from that stern father . . . and that gentle mother . . . to that baby in the manger . . . and I knew—don't ask me how, I just *knew*—that I really was in the presence of God.

There radiated from that child, not exactly a light, more of an aura, of heavenly peace, of divine power, of eternal promise. I felt known . . . and understood . . . and accepted. I felt forgiven . . . and cleansed . . . and renewed. I felt calm . . . yet strong; humbled . . . yet confident; wise . . . but innocent, somehow; centered . . . but no longer on myself.

The silence held. I found myself kneeling . . . and praying— I, who had never knelt to any save the emperor, and had never prayed to any god I can remember! I prayed to the ancient God of the prophets of Israel, who had promised such a Savior; I prayed to the great God who had come to me, so powerfully and so personally, in the birth of this helpless baby; I prayed to the mysterious God I felt filling me with a new spirit of peace and joy and faith and hope and love.

My prayers have only just ended . . . or, perhaps, have only just begun. Others are coming to worship at the manger. The first faint glimmers of dawn are filling the Eastern sky. Above, that wondrous star still gleams. And, in the awesome silence, I, too, listen for the angels' song.

— III —

AARON

("THE LITTLE DRUMMER BOY")

BACKGROUND COMMENTARY

L ATE-NIGHT CANDLELIGHT services on Christmas Eve
    are always a challenge for a serious preacher. Depending
    on the community and congregation, these uniquely ap-
pealing worship events attract "all sorts and conditions" of people: some of whom may never find themselves in a church
otherwise, many of whom have been celebrating the festive season for hours before arriving in the sanctuary, and all of whom
expect something extraordinary, and entertaining, and brief!

It was for just such a service that I first prepared the story
of Aaron—"the little drummer boy"—and for which I have repeated it at least once in every church in which I have conducted Christmas Eve worship ever since. On each occasion, I
have been blessed with a choir and organist willing to play and
sing the popular Harry Simeone song in some way to support
and enhance the soliloquy . . . a fundamental aspect of the power
of this message, I am sure.

Although I never told him so (a lifetime omission I shall always regret), Aaron's story was inspired by my own father, and
his lifelong struggle with the painful lameness with which he
was afflicted by infantile paralysis (as it was called back then)
when he was two years old. Every step he ever took *hurt*, yet he
limped through the more than eight decades of his life with a

dauntless courage and a vibrant enthusiasm I shall always re-member as remarkable. He was always "different"—and he knew it—but he never allowed himself to be "handicapped" by it.

He could have been bitter, but he wasn't. He could have be-come frustrated, angry, mean, rebellious, even violent—all the personality traits my imagination attributed to Aaron—but he didn't. He was a man of faith—simple, deep, trusting, beautiful faith—all the blessed qualities with which, in my imagination, his Christmas Eve encounter with the newborn Lord Jesus Christ imbued the little drummer boy.

As brief as it is, this message has touched many people (mostly men, I realize as I look back on my ministry) who have self-identified with the differentness of my Aaron in one way or another. Psychologists may refer to it as *sublimation*, but men and women of faith seem to recognize the inspiration and abil-ity to transform the negative into positive in their lives as a form of redemption; and, in my book, if a preacher can proclaim *re-demption* convincingly to a candlelit Christmas Eve crowd, that's something to sing *Gloria in excelsis Deo* about!

* * * * *

My best for him

*A soliloquy for Christmas Eve
based on the popular Christmas carol,
"The Little Drummer Boy,"
by Harry Simeone*

My name is Aaron.

You've probably already heard my story . . . or part of it: I seem to have told it so many times. But I don't mind telling it again . . . if you don't mind listening!

To begin at the beginning, I was born lame. My mother had trouble birthing me, and I came into the world feet first . . . with one leg twisted and damaged. Even as a baby, I guess, I knew there was something wrong with me: it took me a long time to learn to crawl . . . and even longer to learn to toddle . . . and by the time I learned to walk, I had also learned that every step hurt . . . unless I was very, very careful.

I guess I was what you'd call a "difficult" child. I was frus-

trated . . . and in pain . . . and aware that I was *different* from the
other children in the village of Bethlehem. And so, as I grew
older, I also grew angrier, and meaner, and more and more violent in temper.

My parents didn't know what to do with me . . . so, when I
was about seven, they apprenticed me to an aging shepherd to
help him tend his flocks of sheep. He was a gentle old soul, wise
even beyond his years, and determined to help me grow out of
my bitterness and violence.

After watching me limp around the sheep-fold for a few
weeks . . . wincing with pain . . . cursing at the other shepherd
boys . . . more often than not flailing out at one of the innocent
lambs that got in my way . . . the old shepherd gave me a present—the first real present I can ever remember getting.

"Here", he said gruffly, "If you feel like hitting something,
hit this!"

It was a drum—a simple little homemade drum with two
whittled sticks. I picked one of them up, and whacked the thing
contemptuously. Iit answered back with the most delicious
"THUMP." I hit it again—harder; another, even better,
"THUMP." I hit it with both sticks . . . but not so hard: "PA-
PA – RUMP!" I beat it senseless . . . and it replied: "PA-
RUMP-A-PUMP PUMP."

I was fascinated—as the old man had intended me to be!—
and, before long, I was not only taking out my frustrations, but
also expressing my feelings, on my little drum. The other shepherds liked to listen to me play—or said they did! (I never knew
whether they really *liked* the sounds I made, and the rhythms I
played, or whether they just liked it that I was hitting the drum

and not *them*!)

And the sheep liked the beat of my drum, too—so much so that they would follow its music, and gather around me wherever I played. I didn't have to run after the wayward lambs any more, and I got to be better at getting the flock into the fold at night than any of the other apprentice boys.

In early winter, after the shearing, it was time to move the flocks farther afield, to the hillside grazing lands that surrounded Bethlehem. Because I was so lame, I was sure they wouldn't let me go along—and that hurt even more than the pain in my leg. It didn't seem fair: I hadn't done anything to deserve all the misery my bad leg brought me! Why didn't God do something about it? . . . if there was a God?

But when the shepherds met together to choose the best apprentices to join them in the fields, they chose me—"but only if you bring your drum!" they warned me. I was so happy! For the first time in my life I was really *happy*!

The trip to the grazing meadows nearly did me in. I walked as fast as I could—and played my drum to keep my part of the flock together—but my leg hurt so much I cried a tear with every step. When we finally camped for the night, I ate a bit of bread and soup . . . and fell sound asleep.

I was awakened by a terrible commotion in the camp. Everyone was up . . . and dressed . . . and shouting . . . and rushing around to secure the sheep folds. Had lions attacked the flocks? Was everybody gone crazy?

Some of the shepherds had seen a vision . . . and heard angels singing . . . and become convinced that the Messiah—the Son of God—had been born in a stable back in Bethlehem. "We're going to see this thing that has come to pass; c'mon! No, on second thought, you'd better stay here . . . you'll just slow the rest of us down . . . and you'll probably never make it there and back." And they were gone.

I was frightened . . . and confused . . . and angry . . . and hurt . . . and ready to burst into tears. With my good leg, I kicked at the closest shadow in the darkness: "BOOM" answered back my old friend, the drum. I sat down and started to play . . . and, as I calmed down, my music gradually changed from raucous to relaxing. The occasional bleat of a lamb . . . the constant murmur of the sheep . . . the mysterious whisper of the wind . . . all seemed to say: "Go along, too; everything here will be all right. The folds are snug . . . the stars are bright . . . the Messiah waits . . . he, too, would like to hear the music of your drum."

Uncertainly . . . hesitantly . . . I set out . . . bravely beating my drum to pluck up my courage . . . and to warn off the lions and tigers that I imagined might be lurking behind every boulder. It was almost dawn when I got back to Bethlehem; but the night was illuminated by the brightest star I had ever seen. I almost thought it was leading me like a heavenly torch . . . so I followed it's gleam all the way to the inn—that seemed as good a place as any to start my search!

I half expected to meet the shepherds on their way back— or at least hear them when I got to town. But everything was deathly quiet—except for a murmur of voices out behind the inn. The stable! I crept round the corner . . . and saw my friends gathered at the stable door—just looking in—as though they were seeing the most beautiful sight of their lives. I was afraid to let them notice me—and know that I had abandoned the flocks in the field: but I was determined to see what they were seeing.

I inched forward . . . knelt down to peep between their legs . . . and shuddered to feel a callused hand grab me by the scruff of the neck . . . and pick me up. The old shepherd stared at me a moment—I dreaded what was coming—then he smiled . . . and whispered "I'm glad you're here" . . . and plunked me down on the stable floor in front of everyone else.

The baby's father looked startled . . . but his mother just smiled as she glanced . . . first at my leg . . . and then at my drum . . . and then at my eyes. "Play," she whispered. And I played! I played my best . . . my softest . . . my sweetest. All my anger . . . all my frustration . . . all my bitterness . . . all my pain . . . surged from my fingers . . . through my drumsticks . . . into my drum . . . and came out beautiful . . . lovely . . . peaceful . . . music . . . fit for a king.

Then the baby glanced my way. I thought I detected a *smile*—though with babies you can never tell whether it might just be *gas*! But what I felt was a blessing . . . a forgiveness . . . a healing—not of my leg, but of my life—not of my pain, but of my personality.

I sensed that I *was* different—as each of us is different from every one else—but for a *reason*. My handicap wasn't a curse: it was a part of who I was, and how I had grown up, and what I had become. It had made me braver that I had known I was . . . and more sensitive . . . and more musical. It had provided me with a gift by which I had been brought closer to God—not driven farther away. My drum and I had praised and pleased the newborn Son of God . . . and my life—and my world—would never be the same.

Nor have they been. It still hurts when I walk . . . and I still rely on my drum to do much of my sheep herding for me. But I am a whole person.

I know that God loves me, and can use me for God's purposes. And I know that I love God . . . and trust God . . . to enable me to cope with whatever pain, whatever frustration, whatever disadvantage, whatever misadventure life puts before me . . . and to rise above it . . . and to fill my life with beauty and joy and peace and love.

What a gift! What a Christmas! What a God!

— IV —

ALPHAEUS
(PART ONE)

THIS IS THE FIRST soliloquy I wrote. With its companion piece (see CHAPTER XV, "In the Upper Room . . . Again"), it represented my long-standing determination to be in my own pulpit on the "low" Sundays after Christmas and Easter, and to offer the stalwart faithful gathered in church on those occasions "something special" to honor their being with me in worship when so many others were not.

The Wyoming Presbyterian Church in Millburn/Short Hills, New Jersey, was the setting for my first solo pastorate. Situated almost midway between Princeton and Manhattan, it was (as I indicated in the *Preface*) almost always in the forefront of whatever was on the leading edge of ecclesiastical life in the nineteen-sixties and -seventies. While I was ministering there, liturgical renewal was coming to the fore in Presbyterian circles: we were "into" chancel drama and dance, lectionary reading and preaching, revival of ancient and traditional worship forms and practices, and experimentation with whatever was contemporary and inclusive in music, art and language. Somehow, from somewhere—I vaguely remember a gift from Dr. John Sutherland Bonnell of an old book of sermon of which I confess I have long since lost track—the idea came to me for a pair of related soliloquies, one for the Sunday after Christmas, and the other for the Sunday after Easter, which would be something special and surprising for the faithful few in worship on those sparsely-attended Sundays.

I wanted to re-tell the Christmas story from a fresh perspective: why not a reflection on the events from the man who told Joseph and Mary there was "no room" for them at his inn? Who was he? How did he feel about what happened, before, during, and after the Nativity? How might he "connect" to the Gospel story again in a post-Resurrection context?

Reading biographies of the disciples and apostles from various sources, I became fascinated by "Alphaeus," the father of the disciple James, of whom there is no clear Gospel mention other than his appearances in the several Scripture lists of the disciples. What prompted my imagination to link Alphaeus' son's identity with the "James the younger" mentioned by Mark's Gospel—and then with "Mary" his mother and "Joses" his brother[1]—I cannot truthfully remember: but, once I did, the whole story, in both parts, virtually unfolded before my eyes!

The King James Version translates Mark's "the younger" as "the less," reflecting on old tradition that *this* James—as compared with the *other* disciple named James, the older twin brother of John—was "lesser" somehow, rather than "younger"—smaller, perhaps, or sicklier, or feebler, or (to put it in today's PC parlance) "developmentally challenged." And that line of thinking led directly to the Bethlehem manger, and the miracle of baby James' survival, not only of a sickly infancy, but even more significant, of Herod's massacre of the Bethlehem infants described in Matthew's post-Nativity narrative.

---

1. See Mark 15:40.

Finally, Alphaeus' musings on the "if only . . ." aspects of his story made for a powerfully indirect form of suggesting "resolutions" for a New Year that would start within a few days of the Sunday on which this soliloquy was first presented.

* * * * *

IF ONLY I HAD KNOWN . . .

Now after the Wise Men had left,
an angel of the Lord appeared to Joseph in a dream and said,
"Get up, take the child and his mother, and flee to Egypt,
and remain there until I tell you;
for Herod is about to search for the child, to destroy him."
Then Joseph got up, took the child and his mother by night,
and went to Egypt . . .
(MATTHEW 2:13-14)

My name is Alphaeus.[2]

My wife and I run the inn across the town square there— or we did until a few days ago, when Herod's soldiers hit town and all the troubles began.[3]

Now my wife and children have run away to my relatives on the seacoast for safety . . . and Herod's troops have taken over the inn as their barracks . . . and I don't know what's going to happen next!

2. See Matthew 10:3, Mark 3:18, Luke 6:15, and Acts 1:13.
3. See Matthew 2:1-18.

The worst thing is, somehow, I feel it's all my fault. You see, I'm a Greek—a Gentile. I married a Hebrew girl about ten years ago, and moved to Bethlehem to take over the management of that old inn, which had been in her family for generations.

We were happy, I guess, Mary and I. Her relatives accepted me, and were kind to us, and gave us lots of advice and encouragement about running the inn. And I became pretty fond of them, and their colorful customs and quaint religious practices . . . although I never made much sense of their insistence that they were God's "Chosen People," and that, some day, their God would send them a "Messiah" to free them from their oppressors and restore them to the glories of the days of their illustrious King David. I guess I never really took the time to hear or study or discuss what it was they so firmly believed. *If only I had known!*

In any case, I was much too busy trying to make a success of their old inn. It's always been a moneymaker: but they never modernized, or expanded, or promoted the place to its full potential. I had a hard time convincing them that growth is the name of the game; and it was only last year that I finally persuaded them to put up the money for a new wing.

Then I really felt under pressure to show a quick return on their investment. But business was unusually slow for a while . . . until the Roman emperor, Caesar Augustus, announced his new taxation system, which required every family in Palestine to travel to their ancestral community to be registered. Bethlehem turned out to be the registration center for all the descendants of the royal house of David—and I realized that I was going to be running a gold mine. *If only I had known!*

The rush began in the early autumn. We became so crowded with travelers that I even moved my wife and children out of our rooms and up to the summer porch on the roof— and made a few extra shekels for ourselves! I was so busy... and making so much money ... and so enjoying every hectic moment of success and power and wealth ... that I hardly noticed the months passing, and the nights getting colder, and my children coughing in their beds, and Mary pleading with me to let them move back to their rooms before she gave birth to the baby she was expecting in a few weeks. *If only I had known!*

With all that was going on, you can understand that I never really noticed that young couple from Nazareth, whom I turned away because there was no room. *If only I had known* she was pregnant and about to deliver. No!—I guess it wouldn't have made any difference!! My own wife was in the same condition, and I wouldn't let *her* have a room!

Apparently, it was my little girl, Miriam, who took pity on the couple from Nazareth—I guess she knew how they felt!— and suggested that they take shelter in the old stable we use for our own animals. Miriam has really been through a lot: she tried to tell me that the Galilean woman was having her baby—I said "That's her problem, not mine!"—so Miriam helped as best she could.

Then, two nights later, my wife gave birth. And Miriam had to help out again, because I was too busy looking after three rich Zoroastrians who had come down from Jerusalem on an errand for King Herod.

My older son, Joses, came to me too, sometime around then, with a crazy story about being out in the fields with his shepherd friends—*that's* the kind of boy *he* is, never around to give a hand when it's needed!—and about seeing a vision, and hearing angel voices, and going to worship the newborn savior of the world. Well, I had no time for that kind of nonsense: so I sent him off to clean the family stable. *If only I had known*!

Nothing really got through to me until my wife sent word to come at once to the summer porch: our new baby son, James, was sickly . . . and near death . . . and she was too weak and ill herself even to hold him any more. I was pretty annoyed—*that* was all I needed right then! But I went, and was totally taken aback by the sight of my wife, shivering on her straw mattress, and the jaundiced little baby, too sickly even to cry, choking for air beside her.

There was no place to move them: the entourage of the Zoroastrian Magi had taken over the whole inn. They had even insisted, I realized bitterly, that the young family from Nazareth be given the best room in the house! Here my wife and child lay at death's door . . . and three *nobodies* from Nazareth were warm and cozy in my best bed. *If only I had known*!

All night, I held little James, and tried to keep him warm. And all night, my wife—and then Joses—and then even Miriam—told me the things that had been going on right under my nose: things I had been too busy and too preoccupied and too cross and too tired to notice: about the shepherds being directed by angels to our very manger to see the newborn savior . . . and about the Magi following a moving star which had stood for days over our inn . . . and about the fabulous gifts they had presented to the baby born in our stable . . . and about the talk around town that God had at last sent His Messiah, the new-born king of the Jews!

Just before dawn, I dozed off into a fitful sleep . . . to awaken at mid-morning with a strange sense of calm and peace. At first, I thought it was just because my family had finally persuaded me to believe in the birth of God's savior, and had convinced me that the love and compassion of God could forgive and cleanse even my guilt and shame over the way I had treated the Messiah at his birth.

But then I realized that the whole inn was strangely silent . . . ominously still. Giving James back to his mother, I rushed downstairs to discover that all my guests were gone. The Zoroastrians had had a vision—or a dream—and had departed at daybreak in a great rush, leaving behind (I'm ashamed to say) a purse of gold worth more than the inn in payment of their account. The Nazarenes were gone, too, supposedly to travel up to Jerusalem to have the ceremonies of circumcision and purification performed in the Temple. *If only I had known* they were leaving: but I had missed even the chance to say goodbye.

Within hours, the ominous hush was broken by the arrival of troops from Jerusalem. It seems that the Magi were supposed to return to tell Herod where they had found the baby: but they had departed another way—and with good reason!—for the king was in a frightened rage, and had commanded every boy baby in Bethlehem murdered, in order to destroy the newborn King of the Jews.

The centurion accosted me in the courtyard. Reports around town had it that a recent birth—under unusual circumstances—had taken place in my inn. My first thought was to deny it. But then a really weird idea occurred to me . . . a truly "off the wall" way to make it up to the newborn king and his parents for the terrible way I had treated them. Yes, I admitted, a baby boy had been born; but his parents were in hiding. I thought I could lure them back, though . . . and, if the soldiers would come to the stable just at dusk, I was sure they would find the baby there then.

In my heart, I wondered whether baby James would live long enough to carry out the trick. I hoped that the soldiers would be satisfied when they had done the dreadful deed, and would stop looking for the real baby Messiah. When I went upstairs to tell my wife my plan, she wept: not for her *baby* (who was obviously going to die anyway) but for *me*, and for the change that had been made in me by my faith in God's savior.

Her tears seemed to give her strength; and she insisted on going with me to the stable, and staying with James, whom I wrapped in swaddling clothes and laid in the manger as reverently as any priest has ever placed a sacrifice upon an altar.

At dusk, the soldiers came. I prayed that they would be easily fooled and quickly satisfied. My wife trembled as the centurion brushed back the straw and unwrapped the baby. Then he laughed—a cynical, blood-curdling laugh: "This baby's half-dead already! Why should we have his blood on our hands? . . . or on our consciences? Let nature take its course with 'the King of the Jews'!"

With that, he tumbled James back into the manger, and insisted I take them to my wine cellar, where they thought they would be more comfortable than in my stable. It was almost an hour before I got back—only to discover that my wife hadn't even moved! Mary sat beside the manger, a picture of peace and repose, gazing down at baby James, lying naked in the straw. I followed her gaze, and saw my son sleeping soundly—breathing regularly—his flesh warm and pink—his tiny fists clutching the swaddling clothes.

Was it the fresh night air that had cured him?...or the all the jostling about?... or the wonder of lying in that manger?...or the miracle of sacrificial love and healing grace? *If only I had known!*

"*If only I had known!*" How often I have muttered those words to myself over the past few days! *If only I had known*... that faith in God and the everyday practice of religion are such important parts of a person's life!

If only I had known... that a successful business and a growing reputation and a lot of money aren't worth sacrificing one's home and family and personal integrity for!

If only I had known... that God comes to us when we least expect Him!—where it is least convenient!—and in the guise of the least likely people in the world!

If only I had known... that children often see and hear and speak the truth we grown-ups miss because we won't watch, or listen to, or share with them!

If only I had known... that God's love really can forgive sin, and cleanse guilt, and overcome shame, and inspire courage, and change lives!

If only I had known... that giving is the only way of receiving—and sharing is the only way of keeping—what we treasure most: even our homes, our families, our very selves!

If only I had known!

— V —

GAMALIEL

BACKGROUND COMMENTARY

IN 1996, AN AUTUMN of ill health intruded upon my intent to offer a soliloquy sermon every other year on Christmas Eve. Earlier in the Advent season, I had commented, in passing in one of my sermons, on the Nativity account as recorded in the Gospel of Luke being quite different from that set out in the Gospel of Matthew, and representing not only an independent oral tradition about the birth of Jesus, but also an alternative time-line of events. This comment sparked an unexpected interest in some members of the congregation, and I decided to begin to deal with the issue in a series of post-Christmas sermons. This monologue about Simeon and his encounter with the Holy Family in the Temple in Jerusalem became the Old Year Sunday soliloquy introduction to that series.

In prefacing the Scripture Lesson for that Sunday (Luke 2:21-38) I spoke to the congregation about the unofficial practice of the non-liturgical Christian Church, especially in recent years, to meld the two different Nativity accounts into one unbroken narrative, and to compress events that may have actually happened over a span of as much as two years into a story that can be portrayed during a forty-five minute children's pageant.

Virtually squeezed out of that "Christmas pageant" scenario has been a cluster of events recorded in the Gospel of Luke as having occurred soon after the birth of the baby Jesus and, in truth, probably long before the "Wise Men from the East" ever arrived on the scene.

In every devout Jewish family of that time, three things would have happened after the birth of a first-born boy baby: his circumcision, about a week later; his mother's ritual purification bath, to cleanse her from the impurity of childbirth and for the resumption of sexual relations, usually a month or so after delivering her child; and the offering of a sacrifice in the Temple in Jerusalem to mark the firstborn's designation as "holy to the Lord."

According to Luke, all three things were done by Mary and Joseph after Jesus was born; and two of them, at least, were accomplished in the Temple precincts in Jerusalem, an easy day's walk from Bethlehem, where our Lord's birth had taken place. These events, carefully recorded by Luke, and by now virtually lost to "the Christmas story," form the background and context for my soliloquy.

Much of what this sermon recounts is based in historical fact, biblical witness and traditional lore. There really was a "Gamaliel" who really was the son of Simeon, and the grandson of Hillel, famous *rabbans* or interpreters of the Jewish law before the destruction of the Temple and the beginning of the local clergy rabbinate as Jewry knows it today. And Gamaliel really was the Talmudic teacher of Saul of Tarsus[1]—and a contemporary of both Nicodemus and Joseph of Arimathea when they served on the Jewish Sanhedrin Council—and the defender of Peter and John when they were brought before the Sanhedrin on charges of preaching a false version of Judaism because they insisted upon the resurrection from the dead of Jesus Christ.[2]

---

1. Acts 22:3.
2. Acts 5:34ff.

But other elements of the soliloquy story come from my imagination—and only one's own knowledge of the Bible will enable one to tell which is which!

* * * * *

MY EYES HAVE SEEN YOUR SALVATION

Then Simeon blessed [Jesus' parents]
and said to his mother Mary,
"This child is destined for the falling
and the rising of many in Israel,
and to be a sign that will be opposed
so that the inner thoughts of many will be revealed—
and a sword will pierce your own soul too."
(LUKE 2:34-35)

My name is Gamaliel. I've just returned from a particularly stormy meeting of the Sanhedrin: I apologize for keeping you waiting . . . but it couldn't be helped.

Despite my pleas, the Council has just meted out a punishment of thirty-nine stripes of the lash upon two of these religious fanatics who call themselves "Christians." Still, it could have been worse, I suppose: there were some on the Council who were so enraged that this man, Peter, and his friend, John, persist in preaching about the resurrection of Jesus of Nazareth from the dead—even after having been thrown into prison for doing so—that the high priest himself demanded that they be sentenced to death![3]

How I miss my father at a time like this!...and how I wish that he were still alive to help me sort out all the personal as well as political implications in what's going on in Jerusalem right now!

My father served as president of the Sanhedrin for a while—back 20 years or so—and, old as he was, and feeble, and almost blind, he was still the craftiest politician I have ever known. A true aristocrat—descended on his mother's side from the royal lineage of King David, and on his father's side from the dynastic family that to this day represents the now-defunct Tribe of Simeon—my father was a skilled courtier in the days of Herod the Great...who was a "king" in name only, and was regarded by the Jews as a puppet propped up on the throne by his boy-hood friend, Octavian, who eventually became the Roman emperor Augustus. But my father was also a great scholar of the Torah; and so he was one of the *rabbans* Herod used to consult on matters of state affecting the Jewish religion.

Although he was a Pharisee, both in terms of his political affiliation as well as his personal conviction, my father was always a very liberal thinker, and raised me to be the same way. He used to say that every point of view ought to be respected, every voice of opposition ought to be heard, because, if whatever plan or program or promise were "of human origin, it [would] fail; but, if it is of God, you will not be able to overthrow [it]."[4]

That was his counsel to Herod more than 30 years ago,

3. Acts 5:17-42.
4. Acts 5:38-39.

when a new fear of Messianism broke out in Jerusalem. A trio of Zoroastrian astrologers appeared suddenly at the royal court in Jerusalem, earnestly inquiring about a child whom they were certain had been born to be "King of the Jews". Herod was in a panic: he summoned his courtiers, along with the chief priests and scribes of Jewry, to inquire about the ancient prophecies concerning the Messiah who was one day to come.[5] Of course, they quoted to him the prophecy of Micah about Bethlehem—*from whom shall come forth ... one who is to rule in Israel*[6]—and Herod, in turn, passed that information along to the Magi.

Sly fox that he was, though, Herod played pious with the Zoroastrians. He inquired about the exact time when the star had appeared . . . and pretended to want to go himself to pay homage to the child who had apparently been born to take his throne away from him and his heirs. No one in Jerusalem ever saw the Magi again—even my father never knew why—but Herod flew into a rage, and gave orders that all the boy babies under the age of two in the whole region around Bethlehem should be slaughtered.[7] The scandal *that* caused, and the disfavor it brought upon him in the eyes of his boyhood friend, Augustus Caesar, turned out to be "the beginning of the end" for Herod, who died in disgrace within two years.

Of course, my father never confessed to the king that he had, in fact, seen the infant object of all this interest—and had actually held him in his arms—in the Temple in Jerusalem a little over a month after the child's birth.

My father was a truly devout and righteous man. He not only studied the Scriptures, he *lived* them . . . and he *believed* them when they promised that, one day, God would send His

5. Matthew 2:1-12.
6. Micah 5:2.
7. Matthew 2:16-18.

Chosen People a Savior to be the consolation of Israel and the light of revelation for the Gentiles.

So he was much taken with the wisdom and conviction of the Magi—after all, the Zoroastrians were the greatest scholars in the world concerning events which might be disclosed in the study of the stars—and he became convinced that the Lord's Messiah had probably been born somewhere in Palestine—perhaps even in Bethlehem—around the time the Magi said. Led by an inner voice of such urgency that it could not be ignored, my father began to go to the Temple Mount every day to watch for a young family to appear for either the ceremonial purification of the mother after childbirth or for the presentation of a sacrifice to honor the designation of the firstborn male of the family as "holy to the Lord."[8]

"When I saw them," my father told me years later when I was old enough to understand the full import of what he was sharing with me, "I just *knew* that they were the ones. And such unlikely ones! A carpenter from Nazareth, with a convoluted claim to the lineage of the House of David, down from Galilee to register for the census with his fiancée—not even yet his wife—so far along in her pregnancy that she gave birth to their first-born in Bethlehem—and in a stable, mind you, not even a proper bed in the inn—because there was no room due to the crowds come for the census!

"My heart nearly broke when I held such a weak, wee, inconsequential thing in my arms, and thought how he was destined by God to be the occasion for the falling and rising of many in Israel . . . a sign that would be opposed as surely as it would be welcomed . . . a word that would cut sharper than a

8. Luke 2:22-24.

two-edged sword to reveal the innermost thoughts of those with whom he came into contact.

"Suddenly, I realized that I was weeping, and wailing, and witnessing to God my faith that my eyes were seeing the very salvation which our loving heavenly Father had prepared in the presence of all peoples—at the crossroads of the world—in the precincts of the very temple Herod the Great had made into a spiritual showplace that drew visitors from the far corners of the earth. I exulted that my God had made good His promise to me, personally, that I should not see death before I had seen the Lord's Messiah:

> *Lord, now lettest Thou Thy servant depart in peace,*
> *according to Thy word; for mine eyes have seen Thy*
> *salvation, which Thou hast prepared in the presence*
> *of all peoples, a light for revelation to the Gentiles, and*
> *for glory to Thy people Israel."[9]*

I can still quote that prayer verbatim—even after all these years—because my father said it every morning and every evening of his life thereafter, until the very day he died.

He said something else, too, that didn't make much sense at the time, but has come to have a lot more significance for me during the past few months. He told how, after he had held and blessed the child in the Temple, he had spoken to the parents, and had prophesied—although it was only much later that he began to think of it as a prophecy rather than just a warning— that the fate of this Messianic child would be so painful that it would pierce his mother's heart like the wound of a sword.[10]

At the season of the last Passover, there was a mild distur-

---

9. Luke 2:29-32.
10. Luke 2:35.

bance in Jerusalem caused by the followers of a so-called "rabbi" from Galilee, one Jesus of Nazareth. The chief priest and his party, and a lot of the Pharisees of my own party, were greatly agitated by this man, and by the power of persuasion he held over the people. They conspired with the Governor, Pontius Pilate, to have Jesus arrested on charges of blasphemy and sedition—the one a religious crime, the other a political one—both punishable by death. When Pilate called the Sanhedrin together to "advise and consent" in the sentencing of this alleged criminal, my friend, Joseph of Arimathea, spoke strongly against the execution sentence, and persuaded me to support his plea for a more moderate handling of the whole matter.

We did not prevail against the majority. Annas and Caiaphas threatened Pilate with a complaint to Caesar, and he caved in . . . as always . . . to their intransigence. The whole Council attended the crucifixion—a particularly gruesome form of execution!—and the one the chief priests had incited the crowds to demand. As Joseph and another Sanhedrin colleague, Nicodemus, stood talking with me about this man, Jesus, and his life and ministry and message, it was as if my dear departed father joined the conversation, too—reminding me of that fateful day in the Temple more than 30 years before—until I became absolutely convinced that the man on the cross was the very same person my father had held in infancy and blessed as the Lord's Messiah.

I could look no longer. I squeezed shut my eyes, and heard myself repeating my own version of my father's almost-forgotten prayer:

*Lord, now let Your servant depart in peace, according
to Your word; for my eyes have seen Your salvation . . .*

I helped Joseph and Nicodemus bury him in the Arimathean's garden tomb. I wondered when some of his women followers, nearly hysterical, described how he had risen from the
dead and left the tomb open and empty. I puzzled when Pilate
and the chief priests put out the story that his disciples stole the
body away to make it look like he had risen. I heard Simon
Peter's sermon at Pentecost, so eloquent that it burned its message upon the memory of everyone who heard it, no matter
where they came from and what language they spoke.

Now, I have intervened with the Sanhedrin not to put Peter
and John to death for persisting in preaching their "good news"
of God's love made known in the life and death and resurrection
of Jesus—good news of forgiveness of sins and gracious mercy
from on high to reestablish a right relationship between our
God and ourselves—something our six-hundred-some laws
have never succeeded in restoring.

I said to the Council—and it was as though my late father
was speaking through me— that, if this Christian faith is of
human origin, it will fail; but if it is of God, then all the armies
of Rome will not be able to overthrow it—and that, in opposing
it, we may actually be fighting against God Himself!

Now I am saying to myself: how does one *know* whether
something is "of God"—or not? How do *I* know whether this
Jesus is *the one* my father thought was to be the Messiah—or
not? How can *anyone* figure out whether God keeps His promises—or not?

Once—and, so far, only that once—I was able to pray my

father's prayer with absolute assurance:

> *Lord, now let Your servant depart in peace, according
> to Your word; for my eyes have seen Your salvation.*

What I saw with my eyes on that cross has never left my
mind ... and reaches out insistently to my heart to make me believe that this *is* the One who is to bring the glory of God to my
people, Israel, and the light of the revelation of God's love to all
peoples of all nations and races and cultures.

What do *you* think? What do *you* know about this man
Jesus? What do *you* believe about your salvation? What do *you*
pray every morning and every night? Have *your* eyes ever seen
God's salvation? ... God's Messiah? ... God's love incarnate in
this Jesus they call "the Christ"? Are *you* at peace with God, because Jesus rose? ... and lives? ... and calls you His own?

You'll have to excuse me: I have a student waiting. Saul is a
passionate young man, which is not unusual in a Jew today.
What is unusual is that he is a Greek-speaking citizen of the
Roman empire, from Tarsus, whose parents have sent him to
me to try to soften the very narrow and hard-hearted kind of
Pharisaism he has learned from his tutors. I want to share with
him what I have just told you ... and ask him some of the same
questions I ask myself ... about Jesus, and the salvation of the
Jews, and the possibility of resurrection from the dead, and the
promise of the light of God's revelation to the Gentiles.

Is all this just "of human origin" and imagination—or is it
really "of God?" Only time will tell!

— VI —

ZACCHAEUS

BACKGROUND COMMENTARY

THIS SOLILOQUY IS A meditation about having the right priorities ... about seeing one's personal situation as over against some of the larger issues of life ... about humility and forgiveness and honor and self-worth ... about God's judgment, God's mercy, God's love incarnate in our Lord Jesus Christ ... and about being thankful for the presence of Christ in our hearts and in our homes. I have frequently presented it when invited to be a guest or supply preacher conducting worship on occasions of either the Canadian or the American Thanksgiving holidays.

Before I read the Scripture lessons on which the message is based, I always invite the listening congregation to prepare their imaginations to travel back to first-century Palestine to meet one of the characters whose story they are about to hear ... without telling them *whose* story it will be until they figure it out for themselves as the soliloquy begins.

Both Scripture readings are found in the Gospel of Luke. The first, from the eighteenth chapter, beginning at verse 9, is the familiar and troubling parable of the Pharisee and the Tax Collector.

In Luke's unfolding narrative of our Lord's troubled trip down from the Galilee, through Samaria to Jericho, and then up to Jerusalem where "everything that is written about the Son

of Man by the prophets will be accomplished,"[1] the second reading follows soon after the first and appears at the beginning of
the nineteenth chapter. It introduces Jericho's real live tax collector—not necessarily the inspiration for the fictional one in
the preceding parable—but who knows!—a notoriously short
little man named Zacchaeus.

It is only in my imagination, of course, that Zacchaeus and
the so-called "rich young ruler" might be related . . . or that Zacchaeus might have been present at Archelais[2] to overhear Jesus
teach the parable of "the Pharisee and the tax collector." But
why not? . . .

* * * * *

1. Luke 18:31ff.
2. Archelais is an obscure village on the West Bank of the Jordan River
north of Jericho on one of the main north/south roads shown on maps of
First-Century Palestine (e.g., *Hammnmond's Atlas of the Bible*, map titled
"Palestine in New Testament Times")—a site chosen by my imagination for
the day's teachings by Jesus described in Luke 17-18.

THE MAN IN THE SYCAMORE TREE

Then Jesus said to Zacchaeus,
"Today salvation has come to this house . . .
For the Son of Man came to seek out and to save the lost."
(LUKE 19:9-10)

So you don't think he should be here in my house, eh! You don't approve of his being a guest in the home of someone you consider to be a "sinner!"

What business is it of yours where Jesus of Nazareth chooses to stay? Did any of you invite him to your house? Not that *I invited* him here: I would never have done that to him, knowing what people like you say and think about tax collectors like me. Jesus invited himself . . . and I am honored, and glad, and deeply moved that he did!

And why do you presume to label me a "sinner" when you know nothing about me but that I am the chief tax collector here in Jericho? You despise me because I work with the Romans . . . and you have shunned me and my family for years.

What do you really know about my life? . . . and my morals?
. . . and what goes on in my heart and mind and soul?

Those of you who saw me up in that sycamore tree this afternoon must have thought that "the old zucchini" had been
out in the sun too long! (I know that's what your children call
me behind my back!) And I know that I have a reputation for
being dignified and reserved—even arrogant—and that my
climbing up a tree in the center of town at noon must have
seemed out of character! But I'm not really as aloof as I act: it's
just my way of protecting myself from the hurts and jests and
insults of people like you.

I was *determined* to see Jesus today. Yesterday I was out at
Archelais to hear him speak. But I'm pretty short—as you can
tell—and the crowd was so thick that I never got near enough
to see him. I could hear him, though: and he told a parable
about two men going up to the Temple to pray.[3]

One was a Pharisee: and I can tell you that Jesus doesn't
have much time for that kind of self-righteous nonsense! But
the other was a tax collector—I couldn't believe my ears—it was
as though Jesus *knew* I was in the crowd. He described *exactly*
how I feel whenever I go up to Jerusalem to the Temple: I feel
unworthy, and ashamed . . . and I can hardly lift my eyes up to
heaven as I pray for the forgiveness of my sins.

Yes, I *am* a sinner—just as we all are—but not necessarily
in the ways you accuse me of. Be that as it may. Jesus ended his
parable by saying that it was the *tax collector* who went home
right with God rather than the Pharisee: because, as he put it,
"everyone who exalts himself will be humbled, and he who
humbles himself will be exalted."

3. Luke 18:9-14.

Then I had dinner last night with my nephew, who is a member of the Sanhedrin—so you can imagine he keeps pretty quiet about his relationship with me! He told me about having had a brief conversation with Jesus yesterday at Archelais. It seems he asked Jesus about the real secret of inheriting eternal life[4]—and was told that he should keep the commandments. My nephew persisted: for he's very righteous and circumspect . . . and still there seems something lacking in his life. So Jesus told him that, if he was really serious about following God's will for his life, he should sell all his possessions, and give the money to the poor, and become one of Jesus' disciples.

My nephew turned away at that—he's very rich, and has many responsibilities, not only to the Sanhedrin, but also to the family. But he's sick at heart—because he knows that Jesus is right: like me, he is so preoccupied with his wealth, and his properties, and his investments, and his obligations, that he has no time for himself, nor for his wife and children, nor for the deep needs of his soul.

So, I just *had* to see Jesus for myself—to see this man who is so perceptive, so compassionate, so wise. I didn't care that it would seem undignified of me to climb up into that sycamore tree: at least I would have a chance to look at Jesus as he walked by! But he didn't walk by. He stopped . . . and glanced at me . . . and called me by name—how, I still don't know!—and, as some of you who were there will have to admit, told me to come down . . . that he intended to spend the night at my house.

You can imagine how I felt. I haven't entertained a Jew under my roof—except for a few of my relatives—since I became chief tax collector. I'm sure that none of *you*—even *now*—

4. Luke 18:18ff.

would accept my hospitality! But here was a rabbi . . . a man of God . . . a great teacher and preacher . . . determined to visit me. I was joyous as I hurried home to give the servants orders to prepare as lavish a banquet as they could on such short notice.

But Jesus wasn't interested in any banquet. He asked me if I could serve his disciples something simple to eat, while he and I sat in the garden and talked. Oh, what a talk! When he looked into my eyes, I knew that he was seeing the deepest secrets of my heart and soul and mind. And when I looked into his eyes, I discovered that I was seeing the mirror image, not of what I *am*, but of what I *can be* . . . of what God *wants* me to *be*—and of what God *wants* me to *do* with my life.

We spoke of wealth and poverty . . . of honesty and cheating . . . of morality and sin . . . of justice and integrity and love and peace and freedom. We talked about the things that really matter to me: my wife and children, our home, our future; and about the things that really bother me: my preoccupation with getting even richer than I already am . . . my shame because of some of the things I have to do to get, and keep, and make a profit on, some of the tax contracts I hold from Rome . . . my anger at the alienation and rejection my work has caused among my friends and relatives and neighbors.

It came as no surprise that Jesus really seemed to understand my feelings; what *did* surprise me was that he began to speak of God's love, and God's forgiveness, and God's reconciliation. He said that God knows what's in a person's heart—that God is more concerned about motives than appearances, and that God can forgive me . . . if I can forgive myself.

I *can't* forgive myself—not without doing a few things to

change my life. I'm going to continue as chief tax collector here in Jericho: I know you won't approve of that . . . because you feel that none of us should have anything to do with the Romans . . . but *someone* has to oversee the collection of the taxes . . . and I intend to be absolutely fair and honest and scrupulous in all my dealings with everyone—Jews and Gentiles alike—from this day forward.

Until I met Jesus, I always thought that I had earned my money fairly and honestly; now I'm not so sure. So, if I've defrauded any of you . . . or if the men who work for me have cheated any of you in calculating your accounts . . . I ask you, not just to forgive me, but to give me your charges, and I will repay you *fourfold*. Some of you will think that I really have gone crazy! Others may suspect that I am trying to buy back your friendship. Neither is true: I just want to set things right with you . . . and with God.

I'm also going to give half of my wealth to the poor. That's not as much as Jesus asked of my nephew . . . but I think it's enough to simplify my life, and to symbolize my determination not to let my possessions crowd out the really important things in my life. I want more time with my wife and children . . . more time to sit in my garden and think about what Jesus has had to say here tonight . . . more time to enjoy the precious gifts of life and love and health and happiness God has granted me.

Today, I am so thankful that salvation has come to my house in the person of Jesus of Nazareth. Whatever you may think of his decision to visit me, I know that it has been the visitation of God's judgment, God's mercy, God's love. I'm at peace for the first time in many years.

I feel forgiven of my past . . . I feel free for my future. I have done stupid things . . . selfish things . . . sinful things—and, because I'm a weak and willful man, I probably shall again.

But I have gladly and gratefully accepted God's acceptance of me—as I experienced it in Jesus' visit to my house—and I am earnestly trying to follow Jesus' lead in showing my gratitude by setting things right in my life.

You still frown . . . and mutter . . . and think ill of me. So be it. At supper tonight, Jesus said that he had come "to seek out and to save the lost." I'm just so thankful that he *sought me*—and *saved me*—because I was more *lost* than ever I knew.

Are you sure he's not *still* searching . . . for *you*?

— VII —

MARTHA

BACKGROUND COMMENTARY

I N THE SPRING OF 1994, I was invited to speak at a Presbyterian Women's Lenten Communion Breakfast in the
First Presbyterian Church of Deerfield, Illinois. For a long
time, I had been wanting to try to write a soliloquy from a
woman's perspective, and this invitation seemed to offer the perfect opportunity.

We had a lot more "Marthas" than "Marys" in the Deerfield
congregation—my own wife, Ann, included! It was she, in fact,
who challenged me to deal with the troubling incident recorded
at the end of the tenth chapter of Luke's Gospel . . . a passage
she admitted had long bothered her, and about which she had
from time to time heard other women questioning or even com-
plaining.[1]

Early in my preparation, however, I became convinced that
I could not deal with the Lukan narrative about Mary and
Martha without also including some reference to the much
lengthier passage in the eleventh chapter of John's Gospel: the
even more troubling story of the death of Lazarus and the accusations against Jesus voiced by *both* Martha and Mary which
ultimately prompted our Lord to raise Lazarus back to life.[2]

In the Johannine narrative, Jesus is depicted as reacting
quite differently to Mary's complaint, "Lord, if you had been
here, my brother would not have died" than he did earlier when

1. Luke 10:38-42.
2. John 11:1-44.

Martha said exactly the same thing to him. To Martha, whom he had once rebuked for being "worried and distracted by many things," he proclaimed the doctrine of eternal life, and identified himself as "the resurrection and the life," challenging her to a profound confession of faith with the query, "Do you believe this?" But with Mary, whom he had praised earlier as having chosen "the better part," Jesus found himself "greatly disturbed in spirit and deeply moved," and "began to weep," whereupon he went to the tomb in which Lazarus had been buried for three days and brought him back to life. The more I pondered the difference, the more convinced I became that our Lord "loved" Mary in a much more emotional way than he did Martha: he was not necessarily "in love" with her—nor she with him, as I have her explain to Martha in the soliloquy—but there was a depth of relationship there that needed to be explored in a different sermon than the one on which I was working for the Women's Communion Breakfast.

That conviction was ultimately frustrated by (a) the audience's reaction to the Martha soliloquy [see below] and (b) the work I began to do on the message that is included in this volume as CHAPTER XII, the poignant post-Easter love story "Who Will Roll Away the Stone?" In creating *that* soliloquy, I came up hard against the form-critical conundrum of the Gospel of John's identification of Mary, the sister of Martha and Lazarus, as being the woman who anointed Jesus at dinner in Bethany and wiped his feet with her hair.[3] The problem, of course, is that the Gospels of Matthew and Mark do not identify that woman at all; and the Gospel of Luke includes a quite different story of what may or may not have been the same

3. John 12:1-8.
4. Matthew 26:6-13, Mark 14:3-9, and Luke 7:36-50.

event[4]—but which was at the heart of the monologue I was developing about a love affair between Mary Magdalene and Joseph of Arimathea.

When I first wrote *this* soliloquy, I did not try to take into account John 12:1-8. Similarly, when I first worked on Mary Magdalene's story, I tried not to have to deal with the apparent Gospel confusion or even conflict. But when I tried to put the two soliloquies into the same summer sermon series of "Transformation Testimonies," I realized that I had to resolve the situation somehow in order to preserve the integrity of my two story lines. The footnote on page 96 and the introduction to CHAPTER XII will show my readers how I tried to do it.

When I first presented Martha's soliloquy at the Lenten Communion Breakfast in Deerfield, the reaction from my audience was tepid at best. Parishioners accustomed to enjoying and appreciating my soliloquies were unimpressed: "You don't make a very convincing woman!" was the gist of several glib reactions. When I pressed for a deeper critique, I frequently heard that my version of Martha's somewhat feminist views on men in general, and on Lazarus, Jesus and the disciples in particular, came across as either patronizing or even *anti*-feminist when spoken by a man's voice.

As a result, I put aside my intention to "do" Mary, and concentrated on the emerging story line that developed into the post-Easter soliloquy that took on the voice and viewpoint of Joseph of Arimathea. I never attempted another monologue from a woman's point of view, and I never presented this one again . . . until the summer of 2006 in Chatham, Ontario. By then, I was remarried, and my bride was thoroughly enjoying the novel experiences of being "a minister's wife!" A trained lay reader in her Episcopalian congregation in Florida, whose "Southern accent" invariably charmed the "Northerners" who lived in Southwestern Ontario, Sherri agreed to present Martha in my stead on the Sunday the "Transformation Testimonies" sermon series brought her to the fore.

The soliloquy was a sensation. At the end of the service, the organist's wife was out of the choir loft like a shot to "high-five" Sherri with the accolade "Girl, you *rock*!" Women of all ages tearfully hugged Sherri and confessed that their feelings about "men" were exactly what she had portrayed as Martha's! . . . and that the "Do you believe this?" confrontation with Jesus as "the resurrection and the life" had probed them as profoundly as if Jesus had been there that morning asking them the same question. For such success, Sherri deserves all the credit.

It is at once humbling and exhilarating to realize that this message, which I could not "put across" with conviction, is probably one of the most powerful of all the soliloquies I have created. It just needs a spokeswoman from *southern* Palestine to present it!

* * * * *

The better part

But the Lord answered her,
"Martha, Martha, you are worried and distracted by many things;
there is need of only one thing.
Mary has chosen the better part,
which will not be taken away from her."

(LUKE 10:41-42)

Looking back on it now, I feel so foolish. But, at the time, I was really *angry*.

Jesus and his disciples usually make Bethany their headquarters when they visit Jerusalem. It's not far from here into the city . . . and they have friends and relatives in town where they can stay. Jesus always used to come to our house: my younger brother, Lazarus, had become one of Jesus' closest friends, and really looked forward to those visits, and the chance to join that inner circle of twelve who were the Rabbi's disciples.

I looked forward to the visits too, but with mixed emotions, and from a little different point of view. Since our parents died, I've run the household as the eldest: and having guests is a lot of extra work. The cleaning . . . the cooking . . . the carrying . . . even one more person makes a big difference—and when that person was Jesus of Nazareth, well, I always wanted everything *perfect.*

And my younger sister, Mary, was no help at all! Oh, she'd give me a hand getting the house ready; but the minute Jesus arrived, she was useless. She'd just *sit*—wherever he sat—listening to whatever he had to say, blushing like a love-struck teenager whenever he looked at her. And he looked at her . . . in ways I didn't much like . . . and didn't much understand at the time. I've got to admit, now, that I was jealous. I was the elder sister, and if he was going to pay attention to either of us, it should be *me*!

It all blew up in my face the next-to-last time they came to Bethany. I had worked so hard getting everything ready for Jesus. We had had to let our last housemaid go—we just couldn't afford her any longer—but I was determined that Jesus would never notice the difference. Mary and I shopped . . . and cooked . . . and swept . . . and dusted . . . and argued . . . for days before. She kept saying that I was making too much of it, that Jesus was coming to see *us*—not our cleaning and cooking—and that less worrying would leave us more time and energy to enjoy our guest, and to listen to his teaching. I told Mary that that was fine for *her* to say; Jesus paid attention to her because she was young and pretty, but I wanted him to admire me for my skills as a homemaker and hostess.

When Mary teased me that the way to *this* man's heart wasn't through his stomach, I nearly slapped her.

We were in that kind of mood when Jesus and his disciples

arrived. They came later than we had expected, and Lazarus had the nerve to invite the whole lot of them in for refreshments before they went off to the different homes where they'd be staying. I was so upset! Right in the middle of making a beautiful meal, I had to drop everything to set out wine and cakes and fruit. Just like a bunch of men! . . . thinking only of themselves, and their pleasure, and giving no thought at all to a woman's plans or preparations!

And just like Mary! . . . to settle herself at Jesus' feet, and give no thought to how I was rushing around trying to serve everyone!

Well, I lost my temper . . . and snapped at Jesus, "Lord, don't you care that my sister has left me to do all the work by myself? Tell Mary to help me!"

But he refused! He told me that I was worrying about too many things . . . that there was need of only one thing . . . that Mary had chosen the right part to play . . . and that he would not deprive her of it.

I was so mad . . . and so hurt . . . and so frustrated . . . that I just slammed down the tray I was carrying . . . and stormed out of the house . . . and swore to myself that I wouldn't lift a finger to fuss over any of them again. "Only one thing"—*indeed!* Mary had chosen "the better part"—had she *really!* Well, they could obviously manage just fine without *me!*

And they *did!* When I got back to the house after a long walk . . . and a good cry . . . and a lot of soul-searching . . . they were gone—even Jesus. Embarrassed by my outburst . . . and by the thought that they had been imposing on me more than they should, the Rabbi and his disciples had left soon after I did.

Lazarus had gone with Jesus to find him another place to stay; and Mary had cleaned up from the refreshments and rescued my dinner from the fire.

All that work and worry had been for nothing! Because of my foolishness, I had lost the respect of the disciples—and the admiration of their Lord. Bitterly, I thought that a woman's place is either at a man's feet, gazing adoringly at everything he does and listening without question to everything he says—or it's in the kitchen, working without complaint to produce on demand the food and drink he takes for granted.

Mary tried to tell me differently. She insisted that Jesus had meant neither to criticize me nor to hurt me . . . but just to make me see things from a different perspective. She claimed that my jealousy was unfounded: that she loved Jesus, it was true . . . but that she was not "in love" with him . . . and that I should try to understand the difference. She said that listening to the words of Jesus was like hearing the Word of God . . . and that, when he was there, speaking about light and love and life as God intends them to be, nothing else seemed to matter for the moment—certainly not refreshments, nor housework, nor setting the table for supper. She explained that "the one thing" necessary about which Jesus had scolded me wasn't food or drink or hospitality at all: it was hearing the truth about God's will for our lives . . . and then having the grace to do it.

I wouldn't listen . . . and I wouldn't let myself even think about Jesus of Nazareth . . . until last month . . . when Lazarus suddenly became sick . . . and eventually died. Mary knew that Jesus was across the Jordan, preaching in Perea, and she urged that we send a message to him that his beloved friend was ill.

Grudgingly, I agreed: what difference would it make?

None! Within 48 hours, Lazarus was gone . . . and it was another four days before Jesus arrived. I don't know what got into me. I was determined to be calm and composed and cordial to my brother's friend. But when I actually saw Jesus coming down the road into Bethany, I ran to meet him . . . and was horrified to hear the first words out of my mouth become a bitter accusation: "Lord, if you had been here, my brother would not have died."[5]

Desperately, I tried to cover my confusion . . . and my anger . . . and my grief . . . and my longing for someone to do something to bring my brother back: "Even now I know that God will give you whatever you ask of Him."[6]

Jesus tried to reassure me: "Your brother will rise again."[7] I had heard the Pharisees arguing with the Sadducees about a resurrection of the dead at the end of the world—but I found little comfort in that! I wanted resurrection *now*; I wanted Lazarus *alive*; I wanted time and opportunity *right then and there* to talk to Jesus more about my life, and my concerns, and my future.

Jesus looked me straight in the eye: "I am the resurrection and the life . . . Do you believe this?"[8]

I wished I could; I thought I did; I answered, "Yes, Lord, I do . . . I believe that you are the Messiah, the Son of God, the one coming into the world."[9] In that moment, it was as though the weight of the world had been lifted from my shoulders. I felt understood; I felt capable; I felt whole; I felt free.

The next few days passed in a blur. I was deeply moved to realize the grief Jesus felt for Mary and me; I was horrified when he insisted upon rolling away the stone from my brother's tomb;

5. John 11:21.
6. John 11:22.
7. John 11:23.
8. John 11:25-26.
9. John 11:27.

but, somehow, I wasn't surprised when his promises about
Lazarus came true before my very eyes. Glory be to God:
Lazarus *was alive!* Jesus had the gift of life for those who be-
lieved in him!

Now Jesus has gone off to Jerusalem to celebrate the
Passover . . . and, if my intuition serves me well, to die. The Pharisees are furious that he has made their doctrine of resurrection
a living reality . . . and they have joined forces against him with
the priests and the lawyers and the collaborators with Rome.[10]

There was a dinner party the other night at the home of our
friend and neighbor, Simon, the one whom Jesus had cured of
leprosy. I mention that specifically, because there are so many
of the Master's followers with similar names . . . and I didn't
want you to think it was Simon Peter who gave the party. For
example, several of Jesus' Marys were there, too, including my
sister and the Mary from Magdala, whom Jesus had relieved of
the "seven demons" of epilepsy early in his ministry.

It was actually she, and not my sister (as some people still
think), who did such a strange and beautiful thing during that
dinner.[11] Mary burst in upon the men who were reclining on
their couches, and anointed Jesus with her bridal perfume—an
act of love and farewell, which Jesus surely understood, even if
no one else did.

We women, at least, are sure that we will never see our Lord
alive again. Yet we're just as sure that he will never be dead to

---

10. John 11:45-53.

11. This reference is an attempt at a conflation of the various Gospel accounts of our Lord's "anointing." In Matthew 26:6-13 and Mark 14:3-9, the
locale is Bethany, and the host of the dinner party is Simon the leper, but
the woman with the jar of "very costly ointment" is unnamed; It is only
John's Gospel (12:1-8) that identifies the woman as Mary, the sister of
Martha and Lazarus; but John makes no mention of the identity of the dinner host. *The New Interpreter's Bible* suggests that Luke's "anointing" story
(7:36-49)—similar in some respects, but quite different in others—is the
earlier account of an analogous but distinct pair of known events in the life

us. He lives . . . in our hearts . . . and in our memories . . . and in our lives. Things go on at home—just the same—and yet it's different.

I'm still the doer . . . and my sister's still the dreamer. But she's more aware of my needs now . . . and more sensitive to the fact that, though spiritual contemplation is wonderful, it doesn't make the beds and set the table.

And I'm more aware of myself . . . and more frank in admitting that a lot of my worrying was unnecessary . . . and unproductive. I was hiding from myself behind my "busyness": hiding from my fear that no one would like me for who I am—let alone *love* me! I was hiding from my resentment that everyone took my homemaking for granted; hiding from my mistaken notion that a woman only exists to please the men in her life; hiding from the risk of being *me*, and of discovering God's will for my life and God's plan for my future, independent of everyone else's expectations of me, and for me.

I'm more spiritual, now that Jesus is a guest in my heart rather than in my home. I take time—every day—for prayer . . . and meditation . . . and solitude. I distinguish between what I *have* to do, and what I *choose* to do. What I *have* to do, I offer to my Lord as my spiritual service . . . and do my best never to nag or complain about it; what I *choose* to do, I accept from my Lord as a privilege and a pleasure . . . and do my best to see that my activities genuinely serve him and others as well as my-

---

of Jesus, each with a fundamentally different set of characters, circumstances and significance. In Luke, the locale is unspecified; the host is unnamed, but is identified as a Pharisee; the woman, too, is unnamed, but is a known "sinner" much in need of the saving forgiveness Jesus bestows on her with the benediction, "Go in peace." The Lukan narrative was the original inspiration for the soliloquy in CHAPTER XII, "Who Will Roll Away the Stone?" I have no evidence or authority for the suggestion that John's Gospel mistakenly identifies Mary of Bethany as the anointer of Jesus, other than to accommodate my beautiful love story that pairs in imagination the two similar events through the lives of Mary Magdalene and Joseph of Arimathea.

self. And I'm more serene—about life and death ... about work and leisure ... about love and marriage ... about friends and family. I do what I must—and what I can ... and I trust the rest to him who is my life ... and my hope ... my friend ... and my future.

What about *you*? Do you "fuss and fret" for Jesus—the way I used to? Or do you really live *for* him—and *in* him—and *through* him—with sensitivity and good sense and compassion and grace? You know, it makes *all the difference!*

— VIII —

SYMEON

BACKGROUND COMMENTARY

BUOYED BY THE SUCCESS of my first pair of soliloquies
for the Sundays after Christmas and Easter of my first
year of ministry in Millburn, New Jersey, I began to
work on a second set for the following year ... and then decided
that an every-year diet of post-holiday soliloquies might prove
to be "a bit much"—not only for my congregation to hear, but
also for me to prepare. It seemed that perhaps an every-other-
year schedule might be better ... and that is what I set out to
do ... not only in that congregation, but also in each of the other
churches I served throughout my ministry.

As it happened, my daughter Sarah's sixth birthday fell on
the Sunday after Christmas in 1970—and I did "something special" that did not involve a soliloquy. For the Lenten/ Eastertide
period of 1971, however, I resumed my intended schedule of
seasonal soliloquies. This one began as a Palm Sunday message;
but Millburn's Director of Music had planned his Lenten musical spectacular for that occasion that year ... and so my monologue "morphed" surprisingly easily into a post-Easter message.

Palm Sunday is one of my favorite days in the Christian
church year. The bittersweet poignancy of "Hosanna!" at the
first of the week turning into "Crucify him!" by Friday has always seemed to me to portend the volatility of shallow faith
prompted more by emotionalism than by commitment. "It's eas-

ier to carry a palm frond than a cross" has been the theme of
many of my Palm Sunday messages . . . and so, for this soliloquy,
I wanted to underline Jesus' call to the deeper discipleship of
cross-bearing.[1]

At the same time, I hoped to indicate to my listeners that
carrying one's cross for Jesus does not always involve dramatic
deeds of self-sacrifice. I believe that we live in God's Kingdom
in the "day in and day out" of our ordinary everyday lives; and
so, despite allowing my protagonist to be an eyewitness to the
Triumphal Entry, I denied him his hoped-for trip to the Upper
Room in Jerusalem, and gave his transformation testimony a
denouement of "never [doing] anything particularly startling
because of [his] new faith." He just tried his very best to live
love . . . and to teach others to live it too . . . which, for me, is a
pretty good description of "the Way" Jesus calls us to walk.

I also wanted to scotch the tendency I had begun to notice
in some of the "yuppies" in my congregation of thinking they
could bargain with God for what they wanted out of life. The
first-century Judaic concept of *corban*, "kept pure for sacrifice"[2]
seemed to me to embody that notion, and "a colt that [had]
never been ridden"[3] (but that was immediately available to Jesus'
disciples upon uttering the code words "The Lord needs it"[4])
intrigued me as an object lesson to that point.

---

1. In the soliloquy, I deliberately reference Matthew 16:24; Mark 8:34;
Luke 9:23 to make this point.

2. *Easton's Bible Dictionary*: A Hebrew word adopted into the Greek of
the New Testament and left untranslated. It occurs only once (Mark 7:11).
It means a gift or offering consecrated to God. Anything over which this
word was once pronounced was irrevocably dedicated to the temple . . . Our
Lord condemns the Pharisees for their false doctrine, inasmuch as by their
traditions they had destroyed the commandment which requires children
to honor their father and mother, teaching them to find excuse from helping
their parents by the device of pronouncing "Corban" over their goods, thus
reserving them to their own selfish use.

3. Luke 19:30.

4. Luke 19:31 and 34.

As the story began to take shape in my imagination, the re-alization that the Synoptic Gospels' story of Jesus healing a blind man—or, in Matthew's Gospel, *two* blind men—on his way out of Jericho is in consistent proximity to the story of the Triumphal Entry began to fascinate me.[5] Somehow, my imagi-nation urged me to explore the story-line possibilities in the per-suasive notion that Jesus could have known (a) that Symeon had vowed to keep his foal corban, (b) that blind Bartimaeus could have been Symeon's brother, and (c) that Bartimaeus could have been trusted to proclaim to his brother—and to my hearers— the theological insight that the Gospel's Jesus in fact fulfils the Law's intentions.

Finally, I had by then been in ministry long enough to rec-ognize that in every congregation there is a cadre of people who love to "spout Scripture" at every opportunity. They enjoy in-terjecting out-of-context bits of the Bible into conversations every chance they get! So, I confess, I have had a bit of fun over the years packing this monologue with scattered references to otherwise-unrelated verses or passages from the Gospels and the Book of the Acts of the Apostles . . . just to see how many such folk would recognize! For example, "Bartimaeus" is mentioned as the name of the blind beggar Jesus healed on his way out of Jericho in Mark 10:46. "Simeon"[6] is identified by James in Acts 15:14 as one of those whose early ministry among Gentiles was cited as exculpatory justification for Paul and Barnabas' evan-gelization of the Gentile world of Asia Minor. The Synoptic Gospels all include the code words "The Lord needs it" as cru-cial to the disciples' mission in securing an unbroken colt on which Jesus could ride in triumph; but only Mark adds the fate-

5. See Matthew 20:29ff. and 21:1ff; Mark 10:46ff. and 11:1ff; Luke 18:35ff. and 19:28.

6. The spelling of which I arbitrarily changed to "Symeon" to avoid any identity confusion with the "righteous and devout" old man who blessed the baby Jesus and his parents in the Temple in Jerusalem (Luke 2:25ff.), giv-ing rise to the Church's ancient hymn, *Nunc Dimittis*.

ful words that prompted Symeon's concern: ". . . and will send it back here immediately" (11:3).

Four years after I first introduced Symeon, my ministry had taken me to center-city Montreal at The Church of St. Andrew and St. Paul. For my Holy Week and Easter sermons in 1975, I decided to rework this soliloquy and another, and to write two more new ones, under the series theme "Famous Last Words from the Gospel of Mark." They appear in this volume as CHAPTER IX, "I Will Not Deny You;" CHAPTER XI, "This Man Was the Son of God;" and CHAPTER XII, "Who Will Roll Away the Stone?"

* * * * *

THE LORD NEEDS IT . . .

"If anyone says to you, 'Why are you doing this,'
just say this,
'The Lord needs it
and will send it back here immediately.'"
(MARK 11:3)

My name is Symeon. I've lived all my life here in the village of Bethphage, out in the suburbs of Jerusalem, on the western slope of the Mount of Olives, near the Garden of Gethsemane.

I'm one of the "People of the Way." The Greeks make fun of us by calling us "Christians"—but we don't mind, because, well, that's what we are—followers of the Christ, *Messiah* in Hebrew, the Lord, Jesus of Nazareth . . . surely you've heard about him!

It was because of him—Jesus—that I nearly had to leave Bethphage, once, a long time ago. He got himself arrested, and put to death, and . . . well, let me begin at the beginning.

I have a brother, named Bartimaeus,[7] who was born blind.

7. Mark 10:46.

He's older than I . . . but he was never able to do any work. Father managed to provide pretty well, but if Mother had been alive—and there had been four mouths to feed, instead of just three—I don't know how we would have survived.

Father died when I was seventeen—leaving Bartimaeus and me with a tiny house, a few shekels, a small inventory of the pots and jugs and cruets he had peddled, and a sturdy young ass swollen with her first foal.[8]

We were desperate: Bartimaeus had often tried to make pottery by feel rather than by sight . . . but his work was too clumsy to sell. I was still too young and timid to be a successful peddler: it would be a long time before my income would be anywhere near my father's!

One day I came home early, my bundle of wares almost as full as when I had left. Salome, the ass, was slow and weary in her "delicate condition": her time must have been coming near. Bartimaeus was packing: "I'm going to Jericho, Symeon, with most of the money we have left. You'll do all right with the pottery business . . . and maybe I'll be able to find work with one of the merchants who are profiting so much from the trade caravans."

The next morning, he left. I was desolate. I couldn't drag myself to gather up those pots and go out peddling. All day I sat at the wheel, shaping, smoothing, smashing, reshaping a tired lump of clay. It's just as well that I didn't try to go out selling, though . . . because Salome seemed wearier than ever . . . and then, at dusk, she gave birth to her foal.

Her firstborn colt: and what a beauty he was! . . . scruffy, but sleek somehow . . . spindly, but very, very strong. A prize:

8. A subtle attempt to acknowledge the mention in Matthew's Gospel account of the Triumphal Entry of *two* beasts of burden—a donkey and a colt—a discrepancy prompted, I suspect, by Matthew's emphasis on New Testament fulfillment of Old Testament prophecy, in this case Zechariah 9:9.

Nathan, I would call him in Aramaic . . . a "gift from God."

Or, maybe, a gift *for* God. A wild and wonderful idea began to form in my mind. I sat in the stall all night, stroking Nathan, talking it over with Salome. Just as dawn was breaking, I slipped through the silent streets to the synagogue . . . and I prayed—as I have never prayed before—that my brother Bartimaeus might be healed of his blindness and be able to come home and work with me in the pottery shop.

And I made a vow—to God the Father of Abraham, Isaac and Jacob—that Nathan, the firstborn colt of my ass, should be kept *corban*, pure for sacrifice, never shod, never harnessed, never ridden . . . so that, if my prayer for Bartimaeus were ever answered, I would have, ready and waiting, a sacrifice worthy of so great a blessing.

Days passed . . . then weeks . . . then months. Every Sabbath, I repeated my prayer and renewed my vow. Nathan was becoming as handsome a colt as I had ever seen, with a silky, silvery coat that glinted almost white in the sunlight.

I really hated to leave him tied to the gatepost, in the cool shade of the wall, while I went off peddling with Salome. But my trips were becoming more frequent: business was picking up—or I was becoming more aggressive, maybe.

My pottery was well thought of in Bethany . . . so I used to go fairly often down through the valley of Kidron to peddle in that area. A couple of times, I even thought of continuing on down to Jericho. I hadn't heard from Bartimaeus in a long time, and I was worried about him. But who would feed and water Nathan? Let God take care of my blind brother: I'd take care of my sacrificial colt!

It was down in Bethany that I first met the Galilean, Jesus of Nazareth, whom I now know to be the Christ. He used to come to Bethany often—oftener than most people realized—to visit at the home of Lazarus and Mary and Martha.[9]

He was quite a man: tall, dark, tanned from being out-of-doors so much . . . but with clear, piercing eyes that looked right through you—or at least so deeply *into* you that they saw all there was to see, and knew all there was to know.

Jesus talked often of God . . . as though he knew God, and loved God, the way I knew and loved my father. And he used to say that God loves us—and somehow I believed him—even though I had always thought of God as stern, and almost angry, judging us for our sins, and demanding of us ceremonies and sacrifices and symbols of our fear and shame.

One day, I told Jesus about Bartimaeus, and about my prayer that my brother should be healed of his blindness . . . and about Nathan, and my vow to keep him ready for sacrifice. For a while, I almost wished I hadn't said anything about it: Jesus told me that he actually didn't think much of people who tried to strike bargains with God—though I had never thought of it quite that way.

Jesus said, too, that there were worse kinds of blindness than my brother's—and that I should be praying for those whose souls were so blind, and whose hearts were so hard, that the good news of God's love could never get through to them.

I began to wonder if loving my one blood brother was enough . . . or if maybe I had a lot of brothers and sisters to love, people related to me, not by blood, but by God, whom Jesus really believed was the Father of us all.

9. See, e.g., John 11:1 and Luke 10:38.

Another thing that Jesus used to say was that he needed people to follow him—to "take up their cross,"[10] he called it once, although it didn't make much sense at the time. He needed people to live the way he was trying to show—the way of love—that's why we call ourselves "People of the Way."

He talked a lot about a Kingdom of Love: that's when some of us began to call him "Lord"—partly to tease him, because a *kingdom* didn't seem a very likely prospect for an itinerant preacher and part-time carpenter!—but partly, though, to show him that some of us had begun to understand that the Kingdom of Love isn't necessarily a *place*, a piece of land—it's anywhere that any of us try to love God with all our heart and soul and mind and strength,[11] and our neighbor . . . not just our own brother or sister . . . as ourselves.

Some of us had begun to feel that we already were citizens of that kingdom—not just the twelve who went everywhere with Jesus—but lots of other people . . . people like me, who only saw and heard Jesus every once in a while, but who had his every word burned upon our memories, and lived as though his very kingdom depended on us.

Still, it was quite a shock that day when two of his disciples showed up at my front door and started to take Nathan away. I was inside, at the potter's wheel—because it was nearing Passover, and no time to be out peddling—when I heard this awful commotion in the street. Over the shouts and arguments of my neighbors, I could hear voices rasping the guttural dialect of Galilee.

I went to the door, and recognized the two men at once. But before I could say a word, one of them spoke out, very dis-

---

10. Matthew 16:24; Mark 8:34; Luke 9:23.
11. Mark 12:28-34.

tinctly, almost as if in code: "The Lord needs it, and will send it back here immediately."[12]

My heart sank. "But . . . but that's Nathan . . . my firstborn colt . . . my sacrifice . . . the Lord knows . . ."

"The Lord needs it . . ."

I shrugged, went back inside, and they led Nathan away.

It took what seemed an eternity for my neighbors to quit their gossiping and drift back to their own homes. As soon as the street was clear, though, I slipped out and headed for the highway to Jerusalem. Something must be up!

Something was! Before long, I overtook a crowd of Passover pilgrims jostling along the road, shouting and singing "Hosanna! Blessed is the one who comes in the name of the Lord! . . . Hosanna in the highest heaven!"[13]

I elbowed my way forward, toward the focus of the demonstration. It was Jesus, astride Nathan.

I stopped dead in my tracks. How *could* he? How could he mount my colt, which had never been ridden, which was corban for sacrifice, which was the only hope for my brother's vision and for my own happiness?

"Hosanna in the highest heaven!" He turned . . . he saw me . . . he smiled . . . smiled as much as to say "I needed him . . . I need *you* . . . citizen of the kingdom . . ."

"Hosanna! Blessed is the one who comes . . .", ". . . who comes "triumphant and victorious . . . humble and riding on . . . a colt, the foal of a donkey." Of course! the prophecy of Zechariah—fulfilled in my presence—on my colt![14]

"Hosanna in the highest heaven!" Caught up in the majesty of the moment, I moved along with the crowd, shouting . . .

12. Mark 11:3.
13. Mark 11:10.
14. Zechariah 9:9.

cheering . . . grasping at palm fronds from the trees lining the highway . . . finally ripping off my coat to make a carpet for my king!

Somehow—don't ask me how—the day waned, and I found my way back home. I was so overcome by conflicting emotions, I didn't even leave the house. What had happened in Jerusalem? Had the people really recognized Jesus as Messiah? Had there been an uprising? Had the Kingdom of Love been established? What might this mean for me . . . and for Bartimaeus? What about my vow, now that Nathan had been defiled as an animal for sacrifice? How could anything be "defiled" for having borne so noble a burden?

I was so distraught that it wasn't until four days later—or four nights, to be exact, because I was in bed at the time—that I remembered *all* that Jesus' disciples had said when they came for the colt.

"The Lord needs it . . ." That was writ large upon my heart, and would be my watchword as long as I lived. But they had also said, "He will send it back here immediately." It was four days. Where was the colt? Had something gone wrong?

A chilling premonition. I was out of bed in a second . . . slipped on my sandals . . . where was my coat? Oh . . . back on the highway, where I had left it on Sunday. Never mind!

"I just know something's wrong", I said to myself. "There's a garden on this side of the mountain: I'll cut through it, and be in Jerusalem in no time. One of Jesus' best friends has a house there . . . he'll know . . .

"What's that? Torches? . . . shouts? . . . soldiers? . . . Judas Iscariot? . . . what's going on?

"They've arrested Jesus! Where are the others? I've got to go to him!"

I started to run toward Jesus. A soldier saw me . . . and grabbed me. I wriggled free . . . but he had hold of my nightshirt. I was stark naked . . . except for my sandals.

It seems so silly now . . . but at the time I felt embarrassed . . . helpless . . . panicky. I ran away home . . . and nobody followed me.[15]

I hid for two days until the Sabbath was over. That evening, I went out for a breath of fresh air. The street, the marketplace, the whole town was buzzing: "Jesus of Nazareth . . .", "that imposter . . .", "that blasphemer . . .", "that troublemaker . . .", "he's been arrested, and tried, and strung up on a cross . . .", "The soldiers of the governor, and the henchmen of the high priest, are out looking for his followers and will have them locked up soon—good riddance, too!"

"Say, Symeon, wasn't that your colt the so-called Messiah was riding during his 'Triumphal Entry' last Sunday? Are you one of them? Better watch out: they'll be looking for you next!"

I fled home . . . and put some things together . . . and planned to leave at dawn—for Jerusalem, I guessed . . . to find the others . . . hiding out, I supposed, in the upper room where so often they had met . . . praying . . . puzzling . . . planning what to do next.

But I never left. In the dark of night, there came a knock at the door—a soft tapping first . . . then an insistent banging . . . then an authoritative grasp of the latch . . . and in strode . . .

. . . Bartimaeus, my blind brother!

---

15. Mark 14:15-52. In CHAPTER XX, I reference this same titillating tidbit of Scripture as identifying Loukas, the young man who grew up to be the writer of the Gospel according to Luke.

"I came as soon as I heard, Symeon. He healed me. I was begging—believe it or not—begging beside the Jericho road . . . and he healed me.[16]

"He's all that he said he was, Symeon . . . and more! He *is* the Son of God: I saw him through eyes that recognized him. Don't be afraid, Symeon: he's going to rise from the dead, just as he said he would. I know it!

"And he needs you, Symeon, just as he needed your colt. He told me he was going to do that—to give you faith in *him* and not in yourself and your bargaining with God. He needs you . . . and he needs me . . . to stay right here in Bethphage, and live as citizens of the kingdom he really has established—the Kingdom of Love."

We stayed.

I never saw Jesus in risen glory, as I might have if I had fled to Jerusalem. I never saw Nathan again; but then, my every prayer had already been answered.

I guess that maybe there's a little corner of the Kingdom of God located here in Bethphage because of me. The church authorities in Jerusalem seem to think so: they once asked me to address a meeting of the Council, and Luke put my name down in the minutes.[17]

But every year, about this time, I go out and walk the highway to Jerusalem. I stand where once I stood . . . I hear again the "Hosannas!" . . . I see Christ smile once more . . . and I know . . . that he still needs me . . .

. . . and that I'm *you*.

16. Mark 10:46-52.
17. Acts 15:14.

— IX —

SIMON PETER

BACKGROUND COMMENTARY

T
HE SPRING OF 1975 was the year of the centennial anniversary of the formation of the Presbyterian Church in Canada. This historic event that was to be celebrated in a Sunday morning worship service to be televised nationally from the Church of St. Andrew and St. Paul in center-city Montreal, of which I was at that time the senior minister. The centennial service was to include a sermon by the Moderator of the General Assembly, and a celebration of the Sacrament of Holy Communion presided over by myself.

Communion services in the Church of St. Andrew and St. Paul were grand and glorious events . . . not just on this occasion of national and denominational significance, but on every quarterly celebration of the sacrament. Two dozen ruling elders, the men in striped trousers and cutaway coats, the women in severe dark suits, carried sterling silver trays of diced bread and thimble-sized individual chalices from an alabaster altar "high and lifted up" at the far end of a Chancel that was almost a city block away from the Narthex doors. A semi-professional choir robed in scarlet cassocks and white surplices sang a *Te Deum* accompanied by one of the finest *Casavant Frères* pipe organs in Canada.

In advance of the centennial special events, I had spent my summer vacation writing and reworking several Lenten-appropriate sermons under the series titled "Famous Last Words from the Gospel of Mark." Because I had not counted on the Good Friday evening worship in "the A&P" *always* being the traditional full choral and orchestral presentation of Handel's "Messiah," and because I wanted to include in the "famous last words" series Simon Peter's ironic boast to Jesus after the Last Supper, "I will not deny you,"[1] I sought the Kirk Session's permission to schedule a "never-done-before" Maundy Thursday evening celebration of the Sacrament of Holy Communion. This was to be a "lowly" event—almost a reenactment of the Last Supper: a simple table set at the foot of the Chancel steps, surrounded by an arc of thirteen chairs (two of which were left vacant—the one in the center for our "unseen host," and another for the traitorous Judas Iscariot). Instead of trays of diced bread, the table bore a gleaming loaf of *challah*, the knotted egg bread inescapably associated (at least in Montreal) with Judaism; instead of sterling silver thimbles, there was a crystal cruet of red wine, and a single large silver chalice for intinction. At the "fraction," I tore the challah loaf in two, and had worshipers come forward from their pews (unheard of in the A&P!!!) to tear off a bite-size bit of bread and dip it into the wine-filled chalice.

But first, to "set the stage" for such a dramatic departure from the century-and-three-quarters-old traditions of that congregation, I prepared and presented this monologue—Simon Peter in the Garden of Gethsemane, musing on all that had been said and done during and after the Passover "last supper" of Jesus with his disciples. Unlike most of my soliloquies and monologues, which I ordinarily present in a pretty straightfor-

1. Mark 14:31b.

ward manner from a pulpit or lectern, I memorized this message, and "acted it out" on the Chancel steps, lounging in fatigue, fighting off sleep, and finally succumbing to the very weariness Jesus eventually rebuked.[2]

The basic story line for this monologue is built on the Gospel of Mark's version of "the night in which Jesus was betrayed"; however, it will be apparent to any Bible student that I have conflated elements of the other Synoptic versions, as well as the details briefly mentioned in the Gospel of John of Judas Iscariot's money management[3] and of Peter's sword cutting off Malchus' ear.[4]

This monologue has proven to be so versatile that I have repeated it in virtually every congregation I have served as an installed or interim pastor—usually on the occasion of a Maundy Thursday Communion service, but occasionally at other times of the year when a "Communion meditation" was required. The familiar Lenten hymns "Alas! and Did My Savior Bleed" and "Go to Dark Gethsemane" make particularly poignant musical brackets at the beginning and end of the message.

* * * * *

2. Mark 14:37 and 40-41. See also Matthew 26:40-41, 43, 45-46 and Luke 22:45-46.

3. John 13:29.

4. John 18:10-11.

I WILL NOT DENY YOU

Peter said to Jesus, "Even though all become deserters,
I will not."
Jesus said to him, "Truly I tell you, this day, this very night,
before the cock crows twice, you will deny me three times."
Bet Peter insisted vehemently,
"Even though I must die with you, I will not deny you."
And all of the disciples said the same.
(MARK 14:29-31)

Ah-h-h... it feels good to be back here in the garden again!
The Master must like this place. He's brought us through
here every night this week on our way back from the Temple to
Bethany. It's a little too spooky for my taste; but in the moonlight, even Gethsemane is beginning to seem familiar and
friendly.

James?... John?... oh, both asleep.[5] I don't blame them.
That room was really hot and stuffy—much too small for a dinner for all of us. I wonder why the Master didn't arrange for a
bigger one? Money, I guess. Judas told me the other day that

---

5. See Mark 14:33ff; also Matthew 26:36ff.

our funds are running pretty low.[6]

I'm sort of drowsy, too . . . but I mustn't let myself fall asleep. The Master told us to stay here and watch . . . although I can't imagine what he wants us to watch *for*. This garden has got to be the safest place in Jerusalem . . . and nobody knows we're here anyway! But after some of the things Jesus said at table tonight—and on the way over here—I'm sure not going to let him catch *me* asleep—even if all the others *are* dozing.

I can just imagine what he'd say: "Simon, are you asleep? Weren't you able to stay awake for one hour, Cephas . . . my 'rock'?"[7]

Some "rock" I've turned out to be! There, at supper, when the Master said that one of us twelve would betray him, I blurted out, just like the others: "You don't mean *me*, do you?"[8]—and I was really concerned that maybe he *did*!

Can you imagine *me* betraying my Lord? Oh, I've had some "ups and downs" with Jesus . . . particularly some "downs." But I could never betray him.

Yet . . . when he said it like that . . . so matter-of-factly . . . I was really afraid . . . that . . . that maybe I *could*.

Oh, that's ridiculous! I wonder who it will be? Not James, certainly . . . or John! And the others are all back there on the knoll. I can see them in the moonlight . . . and I guess they're sleeping, too.

All except Judas Iscariot. But I know it couldn't be Judas. He's gone on an errand. I saw the Master send him out during supper . . . probably for another of these special arrangements we've just been finding out about . . . like the colt for Sunday . . . or the Upper Room for tonight.[9]

6. See John 12:4ff.

7. See Mark 14:37.

8. See Mark14:19.

9. See John 13:27-30; also Matthew 21:1-7 and 26:18ff; Mark 11:1ff. and 14:12ff; Luke 19:29ff. and 22:7ff.

Besides . . . Judas is one of the finest men among us. He's handled our money almost since he joined us. He's honest, accurate, thrifty—impatient, maybe, for the coming of the Kingdom—but a good businessman, and, in my estimation, that's the mark of a good man!

I can't believe *any* of us is going to betray the Master. Maybe Jesus didn't mean it quite that harshly: after all, he's hardly been himself these past few days. Look at him now, up there . . . praying in such distress and anguish. And yet everything is going so well: the twelve of us are behind him all the way; the crowds adore him; the Pharisees and Sadducees can't touch him for fear of starting a riot. The Kingdom's coming . . . I can just feel it!

Still, I wish he hadn't said what he did on the way over here tonight . . . about my denying even knowing him three times before cockcrow in the morning. I guess *I told him*, though: "I will *never* say I don't know you," I said, "even if I have to *die* with you!"[10] And all the others said the same thing, too!

What a way to talk to his friends! As if, should there be a whiff of danger, we'd all turn tail and run for our lives . . . as if, should a Pharisee or a Sadducee asks us whether we're his followers, any of us would say, "No, I never heard of the man" . . . as if, should Jesus ever get into difficulty with the authorities, we wouldn't all arouse the crowds of Jerusalem to demand his immediate release!

Come to think of it, I wish there *would be* a little trouble . . . just to show the Master where we'd stand! Jesus doesn't know it: but I always carry a dagger—a little sword, really. If there were trouble here—right now—I'd whip out my blade and cut a few people up![11] The Master talks a lot about love and

10. Mark 14:21; cf. Matthew 26:33.
11. See John 18:10-11.

peace and turning the other cheek; but, in a bind, I bet he'd be *glad* of me and my sword!

Then again, maybe he *wouldn't*. He's a hard man to figure out. He almost never gets angry with people—no matter what they do to him—he's more bothered by ideas and prejudices and situations that are wrong. Even when he called me "Satan,"[12] he wasn't really *mad* at *me*: He was upset at the idea that I, or anybody, would dare to stand in the way of what he thinks is God's plan for his life.

He isn't even angry with whomever is going to betray him— if anyone is. He's heartbroken to think that *any one of us* may bring such judgment on himself. You know, he nearly wept when he said, "It would have been better for that man if he had never been born!"[13]

And he really *isn't* angry with *me*—even though he says I'm going to deny him three times before daybreak. (Isn't that preposterous!) He took me aside and told me that he had *prayed* for me—knowing what I'm supposed to be going to do!—he prayed for *me* that, even when I deny him, my faith won't fail completely—he prayed that, after I do whatever it is I'm supposed to be going to do—and I still can't imagine it!—I will eventually turn back to him, and be a source of strength to the others—because he apparently thinks *they're* all going to desert him, too.[14]

That's just like him. To see, to know, to understand, in advance, the worst that his followers might do . . . and to go right on loving them, and forgiving them, and praying for them, and providing for them the will and the strength and the grace to turn back to him again . . . and again . . . and again, I sup-

12. See Matthew 16:23 and Mark 8:33.
13. Mark 14:21.
14. See Luke 22:32.

pose ... and yet again.

Maybe *that's* what he meant by the way he broke the bread and poured out the wine tonight—as if it were his broken body and his shed blood[15]—to try to say that we would *always* be *welcome* around his table ... no matter what ... that he would *always* be our Lord ... no matter what!

I'll have to think about that some more ... when my head is clearer ... and I'm not so drowsy.

I must have been sitting here for almost an hour. It surely is a beautiful night ... clear ... still ... a little cool, though ... maybe I'll just wrap my cloak around me, and lean up against this boulder ... there, that's better.

Mustn't go to sleep, though ...

gotta stay awake ...

gotta show him we won't disappoint him ...

we won't deny him ...

ever ...

will we?

15. Mark 14:22-26. Cf. Matthew 26:26-29, Luke 22:14-23, and 1 Corinthians 11:23-26.

— X —

JUDAS ISCARIOT

BACKGROUND COMMENTARY

T HE "LOWLY" MAUNDY Thursday evening celebration
of the Sacrament of Holy Communion I described at
the start of the previous chapter proved so successful
that it became a staple of the Lenten diet of worship in the
Church of St. Andrew and St. Paul. By 1978, I felt it was time
for another soliloquy . . . but, this time, I wanted to focus on
what happened *before and after* the "Last Supper," rather than
during it. Judas Iscariot's betrayal of Jesus seemed a perfect subject.

"*What* have I done?"—and *why*?—is the question every
Christian wants the betrayer to answer. How could one of the
Twelve do what Judas did? . . . and, apparently for a payment of
thirty pieces of silver[1]—the purchase price of a slave! Starting
from the realization that the "thirty pieces of silver" is a detail
unique to Matthew's Gospel—as is the denouement story of
Judas' attempt to return the money to the chief priests, from
whom he had demanded and received it, and his subsequent
suicide by hanging, possibly almost simultaneously to Jesus' own
hanging death by crucifixion—I decided to formulate my
monologue using the Matthean tradition as its basis.

A clue to Judas' real motivation came from *The Interpreter's*

1. See Matthew 26:15 and 27:3, 5-6, and 9. While all four Gospels record
details of Judas' betrayal, Matthew is the only one to mention "thirty pieces
of silver"—an apparent effort to link this element of the Passion story to
Matthew's misquote of a prophecy in Jeremiah. *The New Interpreter's Bible*
indicates that the quote is, in fact, primarily from Zechariah 11:12-13, but
serves Matthew's purpose of focusing, not on Judas' motives in betraying
Jesus, but on the religious leaders, "who appear all the more callous and guilty
by appearing in this scene."

Bible's emphasis on the "conflict of kingdoms" theme pervasive in Matthew's understanding of the developing Gospel narrative. I found myself in increasing sympathy with Judas, and his wish to prompt Jesus to declare himself "King of the Jews" and inaugurate the "Kingdom of God" for which the Jewish people (and the Lord's own disciples) had been waiting so long and so fervently.

Clearly, there is a conflation of all four Gospel traditions in this re-imaging of the texts. Peter's cutting off the ear of Malchus, the High Priest's slave, is mentioned in all four narratives; but the explicit details appear only in John.[2] Judas' self-questioning—"I wonder if [Jesus] had known right from the start?"—came from the brief mention in John 6:71 that Jesus knew that one of the Twelve was "a devil"—and *which one!*—as well as the "dipped piece of bread" moment in John 13:26. The "betrayal" repartee at the Last Supper table is primarily from Matthew: how I wish that in 1978 I had had *The Message's* rendering of our Lord's response to Judas' self-serving question "It isn't me, is it, Rabbi?"—to which Eugene H. Peterson has Jesus reply: "Don't play games with me, Judas."[3] In fact, for this monologue I now quote *The Message* rather than the New Revised Standard Version throughout.

The fundamental thrust of this monologue for my hearers is meant to be heard in Judas' plaintive self-examination: "Have I put what *I* wanted ahead of what *he* wanted . . . ahead of what *God* wanted, for *him* and for *us*?" For me, that is a pretty good definition of sin, and a pretty accurate description of where most of us stand with God in our personal as well as corporate prayer life. When that is *where*—and *who*—and *how*—and

2. See John 18:2; cf. Matthew 26:51-52, Mark 14:47, and Luke 22:49-50.
3. Matthew 26:25.

what—we are, then we are perilously close to our Lord's dreaded judgment "It would have been better for that one not to have been born."[4]

In the Synoptics, there is no Good News of redemption for Judas, even in his remorse. While Matthew's Gospel indicates that Judas hanged himself,[5] by the time the post-Ascension followers of the Risen Christ were remembering the fate of Judas, they were alleging that he himself had purchased the notorious "field of blood" and had committed suicide by throwing himself headlong into it, so that "he burst open in the middle and all his bowels gushed out."[6] I did not feel back then, or have I ever since felt, that, in the midst of a Maundy Thursday Communion service, I could leave the Judas of my soliloquy to that imagined fate. So, instead, I bring him to the point of recalling the admittedly universalist salvation promise of Jesus, the Bread of Life, recorded by John: "Everything that the Father gives me will come to me, and anyone who comes to me I will never drive away . . . for I have come down from heaven, not to do my own will, but the will of him who sent me."[7]

And then, intentionally leaving the issue undecided, I have Judas ask, surely, the very question each of asks at some desperate moment in our own salvation story: "*Anyone*! . . . Could that mean *me*, Lord—*even me*?

* * * * *

---

4. Matthew 26:24; Mark 14:21. Note that Luke mentions the "woe to . . ." but not the "better . . . never to have been born" (Luke 22:22).

5. Matthew 27:5.

6. Acts 1:15-20.

7. John 6:37-38.

SURELY NOT I?

When it was evening, Jesus took his place with the twelve;
and while they were eating, he said
"Truly I tell you, one of you will betray me."
And they became greatly distressed
and began to say to him one after another,
"Surely not I, Lord?"
(MATTHEW 26:20-22)

What have I done?

Nothing is turning out the way I planned. They've arrested my Lord, and taken him prisoner to the palace of Caiaphas . . . and he just let it happen . . . with hardly a struggle . . . as though he *knew* if would happen . . . even *wanted* it to happen!

I was so sure that, when it came to this, he would put up a fight—and proclaim himself our Messiah—and use the God-given powers we all know he has—and win back the support of the crowds—and bring in the Kingdom of God by Passover.

Was I *wrong*? . . . wrong to want things to start happen-

ing? . . . wrong to want him to proclaim himself *now*—when
Jerusalem is full of pilgrims who will fight for him—who already think of him as their king—who are just waiting for an
excuse to turn on the Romans, and overthrow Pilate, and drive
out the garrison?

It almost turned out that way. Just as I expected, Peter lost
his temper when the soldiers tried to arrest Jesus . . . and
whipped out his sword . . . and cut off poor Malchus' ear![8] At
least half the people in that armed mob were *supporters* of
Jesus . . . or at least curious by-standers . . . not *enemies*—I had
seen to *that*! Peter's attack was just what I had told them to wait
for—and they were ready to make a real fracas—when Jesus
stopped it all before it ever started, as though he had foreseen
what I had planned . . . and was determined to prevent it all
from happening.

I wonder if he *has* known right from the start? It nearly
broke my heart to have to face him in the garden a few hours
ago—and to greet him with a rabbi's kiss. (That was the signal
I had worked out with the soldiers.)[9] But it almost seemed as
though he knew what I was up to: he smiled at me reassur-
ingly . . . and encouraged me to do what it was I was there to
do.[10]

Earlier in the evening, at supper, he had told us all that one
of us would betray him to those conspiring against him. The
others were aghast, and started asking incredulously, "It isn't
me, is it, Master?" I was so shocked that he *knew* . . . that I burst

8. John 18:10; cf. Matthew 26:51, Mark 14:47, and Luke 22:50.

9. Matthew 26:48-49; Mark 14:44-45; Luke 22:47-48. It is intriguing that
John's Gospel, while in accord with the Synoptic Gospels on so many points
in the betrayal narrative, does not mention Judas' kiss; instead, Jesus asks
"Whom are you looking for?" and then willingly identifies himself, while
Judas stands silently by (John 18:2-9).

10. Matthew 26:50. Luke's Gospel has Jesus asking a much more poignant
question, "Judas, is it with a kiss that you are betraying the Son of Man"
(22:48)? Mark and John make no mention of Jesus' response to Judas.

out, too: "It isn't me, is it, Rabbi?" He looked me right in the eye, and spoke so softly that no one else heard him in all the clamor: "Don't play games with me, Judas!"

But I *don't feel* that I have *been playing games* with him ... or I *didn't*, until I began to realize how things may turn out. I only meant to *provoke* him into declaring himself ... to put him in so much danger that he would make a move towards Messiahship. Then the mobs would have taken over—the same mobs that practically proclaimed him king last Sunday! They would have driven out the Romans—and put down Caiaphas and his holier-than-thou hypocrites—and won the revolution by the end of the week!

The chief priests paid me thirty pieces of silver to lead them to where Jesus and the other disciples would be spending the evening.[11] I didn't want the money. I would have done it for nothing. *They gave me the price of a slave*, I thought to myself, *but they've bought themselves a new king.*

Now I'm not sure *what* they've bought! Jesus is on trial before Caiaphas ... the other disciples have all run away in fear and bewilderment ... the crowds in the streets are muttering that Jesus is not who or what they thought ... that he is a fraud—a false Messiah—and deserves no better than death. My bag of silver—and my heart—are both as heavy as lead. What have I *done*?[12]

Have I, indeed, betrayed my Lord ... as he said I would? Have I so completely misunderstood him ... after all these

---

11. Matthew 26:14-16. Cf. Luke 22:3-6, which does not mention the amount of "money" the chief priests and scribes were willing to pay. Mark 14:10-11 makes no mention at all of payment. John's Gospel puts great emphasis upon the determination of the chief priests and the Pharisees to arrest Jesus (11:45-57) and clearly suggests that the information Judas provided for the "betrayal" was the location of the place where Jesus often went with his disciples (18:2). No mention is made of any payment for this information.

12. Matthew's Gospel records Judas' remorse, and his attempt to return

months together . . . that I have unwittingly sold him into the hands of his enemies? Have I put what *I* wanted ahead of what *he* wanted . . . ahead of what *God* wanted, for him and for us?

Are the Scriptures he quoted about to be fulfilled—that he is to *suffer* . . . and *die*, as he said . . . and on the third day try to *rise again*? Have our hopes for the salvation of God's people come to such a bitter and hopeless end? Am I he of whom our Lord said, "Woe to that one by whom the Son of Man is betrayed! It would be better for that one not to have been born"?[13]

Has anyone ever been such a fool as I? Has anyone ever so betrayed a friend? Has anyone ever so frustrated the will of God? Has anyone ever so sinned?

Will anyone ever understand me? Will Jesus ever forgive me? Will God in heaven ever receive me?

I keep remembering how Jesus once told us, "I am the Bread of Life. Anyone who aligns with me hungers no more and thirsts no more. . . . Every person the Father gives me eventually comes running to me. And once that person is with me, I hold on and don't let go . . . This is what my Father wants: that *anyone* who sees the Son and trusts who he is and what he does and then aligns with him will enter *real* life, *eternal* life."[14]

Anyone! . . . Could that mean *me*, Lord . . . *even me*?

the "thirty pieces of silver" to the chief priests and the elders. Typically, Matthew discerns a fulfillment of Old Testament prophecy in the use of Judas' bribe money to buy *akeldama*, "the Field of Blood" also known as "the potter's field" (27:3-10), supposedly a prophecy from Jeremiah but actually more likely from Zechariah 11:12-13. Matthew is the only Gospel to mention Judas' subsequent suicide, although the writer of Luke and Acts clearly knew the details of Judas' fate, but did not choose to make mention of the suicide within his Passion narrative.

13. Matthew 26:24. Again, *The Message* renders Jesus' threatening warning with so much more contemporary clarity and power: ". . . better never to have been born than to do this!"

14. John 6:35, 37, and 39-40 from *The Message*.

— XI —

PONTIUS PILATE

BACKGROUND COMMENTARY

THIS SOLILOQUY BEGAN as the third in a series of four
Lenten/Easter messages I planned and prepared for a
1975 sermon series to be titled "Famous Last Words
from the Gospel of Mark." It was to have been a monologue for
Good Friday inspired by the centurion's confession of faith following the crucifixion of Jesus, "Truly this man was [the] son
of God!"[1]

As I have already written in the Background Commentary
to CHAPTER IX, unexpected scheduling factors intruded themselves into my plans, among them the realization that there
would be no Good Friday worship service in the Church of St.
Andrew and St. Paul during which I could present this message.
As things turned out, I was that year invited to preach at one of
the Lenten Sunday evening services held in St. James United
Church farther downtown in Montreal. I decided not to let this
already-written monologue go to waste, so I planned to present
it—and, in fact, I did!—on that occasion. "That occasion"
turned out to be a bitterly cold, snowy, horrid evening in Montreal, and only a handful of people showed up for the service,
including almost no one from my own congregation!

My projected *magnum opus* for Easter that year was to be
the culmination of the "Famous Last Words" series, a message
based on the women's question as they went to Jesus' tomb,

1. Mark 15:39, RSV. The New Revised Standard Version was not published until 1989, by which time the soliloquy had abandoned its connection
to the sermon series, "Famous Last Words from the Gospel of Mark," and
had assumed the title "What Shall I Do with Him?" based on Pontius Pilate's
question in Mark 15:12.

"Who Will Roll Away the Stone?"[2] But that soliloquy was just not "coming together" for me at that time. I had never done a monologue using a woman's voice (a reticence I overcame unfortunately, remember, when years later I essayed a sermon from the point of view of Martha, the sister of Mary and Lazarus, with less than satisfactory results!)[3] And I was already wrestling in imagination with an unfolding love-story-line involving Mary Magdalene and Joseph of Arimathea—a story that would not be hurried, and only became an Easter soliloquy four years later.[4]

So Pontius Pilate showed up in my pulpit that Easter morning in 1975, and caused quite a stir. The questions with which I concluded the message seemed to "hit home" with profound power in an overflow congregation of "Christmas and Easter" Christians for many of whom faith might have been anything but profound!

Over the years since, I have reworked this monologue with slightly different time references to make it appropriate for whichever of the Eastertide occasions on which I was to present it. As recently as Easter 2007 Pontius Pilate was to appear at a non-denominational outdoor early-Easter-morning community worship event in WaterColor, Florida—but got "rained out" by a freakish early April sleet storm. To my amazement, "word of mouth" advance notice of my intent to present a soliloquy on this occasion prompted a large group of rain-soaked worshipers to gather in a sheltered breezeway at the Inn to ask me to introduce Pontius Pilate *anyway*! . . . which I felt truly honored to do.

* * * *

2. Mark 16:3.
3. See CHAPTER VII, "The Better Part."
4. See CHAPTER XII, "Who Will Roll Away the Stone?"

WHAT SHALL I DO WITH HIM?

This has to be the Son of God!
(MARK 15:39)[5]

"This has to be the Son of God!"

My centurion wrote that—or rather, said it—and then repeated it in this written report of all that's been happening around here this weekend.[6]

I've just been reading over that report . . . again . . . and I confess I'm very, very troubled. Let me tell you about it.

Passover is always difficult in Judea . . . so every year around now I come down from Caesarea to take personal command of the garrison stationed here in Jerusalem in this imposing Anto-

---

5. Despite my generally consistent use of the New Revised Standard Version as the source of my Scripture quotes, for this soliloquy I have come to prefer the renderings of *The Message* so strongly that I have reworked each reference to read as Eugene H. Peterson has paraphrased it.

6. Mention of the timing of the crucifixion relative to the preaching of the sermon has become a variable I adjust depending on the circumstances in which I am delivering this particular message.

nia Fortress.

This time, almost as soon as I arrived, Caiaphas, the Jewish high priest, and Annas, his father-in-law, came to see me. They were terribly worked up about some Galilean they referred to as "Jesus of Nazareth," who they claimed was stirring up their people by his preaching, and who had been given a tumultuous ovation the day before by a huge crowd of Passover pilgrims.[7]

They made me promise—and, frankly, I was willing to promise them just about *anything* to keep the peace—that, if they could arrest and try this Jesus, I would sentence him according to their Law.

I didn't think of it again ... until early Friday morning ... when they, and a surly mob, brought this proud and pathetic man to my seat of judgment at the palace portico. They accused this Jesus of blasphemy—of saying he was their "Messiah," the Son of their God. They accused him of "subverting their nation"—of stirring up the people against their established religion. And then, even worse, they accused him of "sedition"—of proclaiming Himself to be "King of the Jews."[8]

I hardly took them seriously. Their prisoner was obviously so harmless, so meek, so humble, so unaggressive ... and yet ... and yet, he was strong, too, and almost noble, and seemed to be judging *me* at the very moment I was judging *him.*

He wouldn't answer "yes" or "no" to any of my questions. Finally, in exasperation, I asked him, "*Are* you the 'King of the Jews'?"[9]

---

7. Jesus' "Triumphal Entry" into Jerusalem is recorded in Matthew 21:1-11, Mark 11:1-10, and Luke 19:28-40. John's Gospel also refers to this "Palm Sunday" turning-point event (12:12-19) but places it on a different time-line, much earlier in Jesus' public ministry.

8. The charges against Jesus as summarized in Luke's Gospel (23:1-5). Similar accusations are recorded by Matthew 27:1-2 and 11-14, Mark 15:1-5, and John 18:28-38.

9. Matthew 27:11, Mark 15:2, Luke 23:3, and John 18:37.

His unforgettably ambiguous reply: "If you say so."[10]

I really couldn't find anything on which to convict him ... and the chief priests were obviously so emotional about the whole thing that their charges were clearly more hatred than fact. How could I wriggle out of this power play?

I had an idea. There were three rabble-rousers in the fortress dungeon, sentenced and waiting to be crucified. One of them had the same first name as the accused ... "Jesus" ... Jesus, son of Abbas. Now, *he* was a *real* troublemaker. Since tradition demanded that I release to the people a prisoner of their choice at Passover, I'd offer them Jesus *Bar-Joseph* or Jesus *Bar-Abbas*. No one in his right mind would choose Bar-Abbas![11]

But they *did*! "So what do I do with this man you call King of the Jews?"

"Do what you were going to do with Bar-Abbas: nail him to a cross!"

I hadn't expected it to come to *that*. "But for what crime? I've found nothing in him deserving death!"[12]

"Nail him to a cross! Crucify him!" they shouted all the more.

I shook my head, and went inside. I was beginning to feel trapped. Caiaphas followed me ... and suggested, "If you par-

10. *The Message*'s brilliant rendering of Jesus' enigmatic response to Pilate's query in Matthew 27:11, Mark 15:2, and Luke 23:3. John's Gospel records a longer and much more theologically provocative exchange between Pilate and Jesus at this point (18:37-38). Despite my generally consistent use of NRSV wordings, it is the pithy insight of Eugene H. Peterson's paraphrase here that originally persuaded me to quote it exclusively in this sermon!

11. Pilate's attempt to release Jesus according to the Passover custom, and the crowd's insistence upon the release of Jesus Barabbas (Matthew 27:15-22) is included in all four Gospel Passion narratives. See also Mark 15:6-14, Luke 23:13-24, and John 18:39-40.

12. Luke 23:22. The Gospels of Matthew and Mark make no clear mention of Pilate's efforts to exonerate Jesus before the crowd. John's Gospel emphasizes Pilate's dilemma and attempts to avoid sentencing Jesus to death (18:31, 38 and 19:4, 6, 12, and 15).

don this man, you're no friend of Caesar's! Anyone setting himself up as a 'king' defies Caesar!"[13]

I hadn't figured on *that* attack! I knew I was already in enough trouble in Rome, without there going back a report that I was "soft" on traitors. And what was this Jesus to *me*? . . . *why not* crucify him in Bar-Abbas' place?

Then a servant handed me a note from my wife, Claudia. "Don't get mixed up in judging this innocent man. I've been through a long and troubled night because of a dream about him."[14] Outside the mob had taken up a chant: "Crucify! . . . Crucify! . . . Crucify! . . ."

How was I going to get out of this with my reputation . . . and my authority . . . and, indeed, my *life*?

Perhaps a touch of melodrama was what the situation needed. I had a basin taken out to the portico, by the seat of judgment, and I went out and washed my hands before the crowd. There came a great hush! I knew it wasn't altogether true, but I said "I'm washing my hands of responsibility for this man's death. From now on, it's in your hands . . ."[15]

They roared and cheered in reply: "We'll take the blame, we and our children after us." So I signaled the guards to whip him and take him away to be crucified.

This wasn't the end of it—though I wish it had been. Late that afternoon, the centurion of the garrison—the one who wrote this report—burst in on me, shouting and sobbing: "We're all *doomed*, Pilate: you and me and all of us—this man has to be the Son of God!"

13. John 19:12. Only John's Gospel includes this insidious "twist" to Pilate's problems in trying not to sentence Jesus to death.

14. Matthew 27:19. Only Matthew's Gospel records this intimate glimpse into what was going on in Pilate's mind as he wrestled with the dilemma of sentencing Jesus. This detail is Matthew's only concession to lessening the blame he imputes to Pilate for Jesus' death.

15. Matthew 27:24. Again, only Matthew's Gospel records this bit of melodrama.

I had hardly regained my composure when one of the members of the Sanhedrin, a Joseph, (the one from Arimathea, I think) arrived to ask for permission to remove Jesus' body from the cross for burial before sunset. In view of all that had happened, I thought it wise to send along a detail of soldiers to accompany Joseph, to supervise the burial, and to guard the tomb against vandals.[16]

That *still* wasn't the end of it. On the third day, early this morning, while I was still in bed, I was awakened by Petronius, the leader of the guard at the tomb. He was terrified—practically incoherent—but I gathered that, at dawn, there had been a thundering noise at the gravesite, and a blinding light . . . and that, by the time the guards had recovered themselves, the rock sealing the tomb had been rolled away, and the tomb was empty.

It was *my* turn to be terrified. What was I involved in? What would the chief priests say when they found out? They'd never believe my soldiers' story . . . they'd probably start a riot over Roman incompetence . . . maybe even stone the soldiers . . . and get me dismissed!

But, it turned out, my men had already been to Caiaphas . . . and he had wisely told them to forget their crazy story about thunder and lightning . . . and to tell me—and anybody else who asked—that they had simply fallen asleep, been overpowered by a mob of Jesus' followers, and watched, helpless, while the Galilean's disciples had opened the tomb and stolen the body away.

In fact—and you can imagine my surprise—when I questioned Petronius and his men more closely, they were all smiles,

16. The request of Joseph of Arimathea to remove Jesus' body from the cross and bury it in his own new-hewn tomb is attested in all four Gospels (Matthew 27:57-61, Mark 15:42-47, Luke 23:50-56, and John 19:38-42), although the details of who was also present, the stone that was rolled to seal the tomb, and the assignment of the guards differ from one account to another.

and all richer than when they had gone on duty the night before last!

Apparently Caiaphas is delighted with their trumped-up story, and wants them to repeat it as widely as possible. It seems that Jesus had more than once prophesied that he would "be raised from the dead" on the third day. The high priests of the Jews have been waiting with fear and trepidation to see if that prophecy might come true—which, God forbid, it sounds as though it *has*!—so they're putting the best possible face on it, and pretending to be shocked to have been told that Jesus' disciples have staged a grave robbery to make it seem so.[17]

I'm probably the only one in Jerusalem who knows the *true* story . . . and it's beginning to haunt me! Maybe my centurion was right—maybe this Jesus truly *was* the Son of God—and we have put him to death! Before I leave for Caesarea, I'm going to have to find out more.

But . . . what could I have done *differently*? What *should* I have done with Jesus? What would *you* have done, if you had been in my place . . . or if you had been there in that courtyard with the crowd yelling at me?

Have you ever felt *trapped* like that? . . . trapped by the pressure of what other people want you to do? . . . trapped by the danger of losing your job? . . . trapped by the distractions of your private concerns? . . . trapped by the threats of those *around* you to tell those *above* you that you're not their *friend*?

What *would* Jesus have been to you then? . . . what *would* you have done? . . . what would you have had *me* do? . . . what would you have *shouted* above the crowd when I asked, "What shall I do with him?"

---

17. Only Matthew's Gospel tells this story of the denouement of Jesus' burial and resurrection (28:11-15). The Gospel writer's concern to proclaim the Good News to a Jewish audience makes this narrative important as counter-evidence to the "story still told among the Jews to this day."

And—what *should* I do with him? . . . and the *truth* about him? . . . even *now*? . . .

And—what will *you* do with him? . . . and about him? . . . when he stands before you in your moment to decide? Think about it!!!

— XII —

JOSEPH OF ARIMATHEA

BACKGROUND COMMENTARY

T HIS IS A SURPRISING love story, weaving together a
cluster of Scripture passages . . . some very familiar, others not so. Whenever I present it, I always precede it
with the caveat that the fictional thread connecting the passages
of Scripture on which it is based is strictly the work of my imagination: there is no direct Biblical basis for what I have created.

Nevertheless, I have boldly offered it to my several congregations as my way of retelling the Easter story so as to help even
casual Christians feel as though "they were there"—and to help
them understand what it must have been like to live through a
time that changed the course of human history. Again and
again, I have invited my listeners to travel back in imagination
to the first century of the Common Era . . . to Jerusalem . . . to
a palatial townhouse with a walled garden . . . to meet the man
who buried Jesus.

The monologue is grounded primarily in passages found in
the Gospel according to Mark. In worship, I start the Scripture
Lesson(s) with the late afternoon of what we call Good Friday—at Mark 15:42—and then continue reading right through
the Easter narrative to the end of Mark 16:8.

But my "back story" of the developing love affair between
Mary Magdalene and Joseph of Arimathea draws from a variety
of Gospel sources, and focuses on a resolution of the notoriously

troubling and apparently contradictory doublet of similar (if not virtually identical) accounts of what happened at a dinner at an unnamed Pharisee's house[1] and again at another dinner at a home in Bethany,[2] during both of which a woman rightly or wrongly identified as "a sinner" washed Jesus' feet with her tears and anointed them with costly perfumed ointment.

In the background commentary to CHAPTER VII, I have described the fiction with which I tried to resolve the question of whether that "woman" was Mary Magdalene[3] or Mary the sister of Martha and Lazarus.[4] As part of this imaginary resolution, I think that Joseph of Arimathea's gifts of containers of costly nard on two different occasions serves me well, and underscores the length and depth of his devotion to Mary of Magdala— which sentiment also convincingly accounts for the motivation of this otherwise unknown follower of Jesus to appear with Nicodemus to claim the crucified body of Mary's beloved rabbi for burial in his newly hewn family tomb on the outskirts of Jerusalem.[5]

In my monologue, Joseph's reflections on the physical mechanics of rolling the tombstone one way or another have been profoundly affected and eventually reinterpreted after my several visits to "the Garden Tomb" tourist site maintained in Jerusalem to this day by evangelical Christian volunteers from England and the British Commonwealth. Once one sees that purported gravesite, and the huge round stone leaning against

---

1. Luke 7:36-50.

2. See Matthew 26:6-13, Mark 14:3-9, and John 12:1-8, each of which includes details not mentioned by the others, and all of which I have conflated into my fictionalized rationalization of who was involved and what might have happened.

3. The traditional assumption associated with the account in Luke 7:36ff.

4. Although clearly stated in John 12:3, this identification is not mentioned in either Matthew 26:7 or Mark 14:3, which omission, I felt, gave me some literary license to impose another resolution onto the question.

5. In CHAPTER XIII, "Mistaken Identity," I explore further the relation-

the cliffside nearby, one can never again ignore the poignant reality of the anticipated problem for the women on their way to
embalm Jesus' body, and the astonishing persuasiveness of the
Gospel accounts of where and how the Lord's grave-clothes
were found after the Resurrection.

* * * * *

ship between Joseph of Arimathea and Nicodemus in another post-Easter
meditation on first-hand experiences of the Risen Lord.

Who will roll away the stone?

The women had been saying to one another,
"Who will roll away the stone for us from the entrance to the tomb?"
When they looked up, they saw that the stone,
which was very large, had already been rolled back.

(MARK 16:3-4)

Thank you for coming. . . and for waiting. I never dreamt I would be at the Governor's palace so long. So many dangerous questions. . . so many dangerous answers. I hope I said the right things—for Mary's sake.

It's really been quite a weekend around here. I'm so bewildered and confused—I don't know what to think . . . or even where to start thinking. Perhaps it would help me sort out my thoughts if I told you about Mary: do you mind?

Mary's going to be my bride . . . I hope.

Things have never been easy for Mary. She grew up in the Galilee, in the village of Magdala, a dreary little place between Nazareth and Capernaum. Her parents were drowned in a boating accident when she was four, and she was bounced around from relative to relative.

She grew up to be very beautiful, very independent, and very tense. She also suffered from epilepsy—"the disease of the seven demons," the ignorant people call it—and lived in daily fear of what she might do to herself. Because of her unusual beauty... and, at times, her even more unusual behavior... people misjudged her, and thought her to be willful and wicked, which she wasn't at all!

I fell in love with her the first time I saw her. It was at a wedding reception in Cana.[6] One of my cousins was being married. His brother, Nathanael,[7] had become a disciple of Jesus of Nazareth—surely you've heard about *him* in the past few days! Well, Nathanael had invited this Jesus and his followers to the wedding feast. I didn't know it at the time, but Jesus had healed Mary of her epilepsy just days before,[8] and she had joined the band of people who traveled with the so-called "Rabbi," ministering to the poor and sick and underprivileged.

I only spoke to her long enough to find out her name... and where she was staying... and she was off. There was a problem with the refreshments—because of so many unexpected guests—and she wanted to be of help.

Immediately, I dispatched a servant home to Arimathea. My family grows and processes the finest and costliest herbs and ointments and perfumes in Palestine, and I wanted him to fetch back the gift for which we and our estate have become famous... an exquisite alabaster jar[9] filled with the most fragrant essence of nard... to be delivered with my compliments to the lovely Mary of Magdala.

6. John 2:1-11.

7. John 21:2.

8. Luke 8:2.

9. Luke 7:37 mentions the alabaster jar; the "nard" detail comes from John 12:3.

She never acknowledged the gift. I ached for some word, some response, some encouragement: *nothing*—for two years—*nothing*! And then, we met again—by chance, perhaps, or by providence. My good friend and business associate, Nicodemus, invited me to a dinner party at his villa outside Jerusalem . . . to meet a rabbi, he said, who had made a profound impact on his life.[10]

It turned out to be Jesus, the same Jesus I had seen briefly at the wedding in Cana. My heart leapt. Might *she* be? . . . she *was* . . . among the guests . . . and she *remembered* me!

For almost a year, I courted her—on and off, because she insisted on trooping around the countryside with the followers of Jesus—and thought I was getting nowhere. Time and again, I asked her to marry me—and then, one day, out of the clear blue sky, she said "Yes."

She told me that I owed her change of heart to Jesus. He had confided to her that he didn't expect to be out around the country preaching much longer—and that he wanted to see her settle down with a home and a husband and a hope for the future.

What a proud and happy man I was! That very day, my servant was on his way to Arimathea to bring back some of my family's heirloom jewelry for my bride-to-be . . . and another alabaster jar of ointment—for sentimental reasons, partly—and partly because Mary had never ever mentioned that first gift, and I was curious to find out what she had done with it.

My servant returned on the evening of our engagement announcement party. One of Mary's closest friends, a man named Simon, who lived in Bethany and had been healed of leprosy by

10. John 3:1-21.

Jesus, was giving a dinner for us[11]—a most unusual thing—but then, they were an unusual fellowship, those followers of Jesus.

Before we made the formal announcement, I gave Mary the jewelry and the perfumed ointment. She was pleased by the jewels—naturally—but obviously troubled by the perfume. "What did you do with the first jar?" I whispered.

She smiled a strange, pained, uncomfortable smile. "I'll show you what I've never told you . . . and I hope you'll understand."

Swiftly, silently, she got up from her place, moved to where Jesus was sitting, broke open the jar, and poured its priceless contents on her master's head.[12] As the pungent aroma of the nard filled the room, there was a growing murmur among the guests.

Some of us recognized in Mary's gesture the thrilling symbolism of the age-old ceremony of anointing a king of Israel—as Samuel had done for Saul . . . and Zadok for Solomon . . . and Elisha for Jehu—and we understood that this was her way of saying that she believed Jesus to be the Messiah of prophecy, and the promised Kingdom of God to be on its way![13]

But there were others who saw things differently. "What was the use of wasting all that perfume again? It was worth at least a year's wages. It could have been *sold*, and the money given to the poor!"

Jesus was furious. "Leave her alone! Why are you bothering her? She has done a fine and beautiful thing for me. She did what she thought was right. Whether she knew it or not, she has poured perfume on my body to prepare it for burial ahead of time."

11. Mark 14:3ff.
12. John 12:1ff; cf. Luke 7:36-38.
13. Cf. I Samuel 10:1, I Kings 1:38-9, and II Kings 9:4-10.

For burial? . . . not for kingship? A deathly hush fell over the room. Without a word, Jesus got up and left. I never saw him alive again. Mary and I left, too; the party was over, and it didn't really matter that our engagement was still unannounced.

"She poured perfume on my body to prepare it for burial ahead of time . . ." The words of Jesus were ringing in Mary's ears, and echoing in her heart.

"He really believes it, Joseph," she said to me at the door of the house where she was staying, "he really believes he's going to be put to death—and soon.

"Joseph, make me a promise—a betrothal promise—please. You're not one of his followers, I know . . . and you've never approved of my going off on his preaching missions . . . but he means everything to me, Joseph. If he should die . . . soon . . . will you make arrangements for his burial?

"There's a tomb out in the garden of your town house here in Jerusalem—a new one—I saw the workmen digging it. And there must be a family mausoleum at Arimathea. Whenever it happens . . . if ever . . . wherever . . . will you . . . for me?"

Well, it happened—just this weekend—sooner than anybody expected.

I took Nicodemus with me to ask permission of the Governor to bury Jesus. Pilate was certainly surprised to have two of the richest men in Jerusalem come to claim the body of someone he had just sentenced to death by crucifixion as a common criminal![14]

Mary was still at the cross, with two other women, when we arrived at Golgotha. I had brought a length of linen. We wrapped the body tightly, carried it over the hill to my garden—

---

14. Mark 15:42ff; cf. John 20:39.

it wasn't very far—and laid it to rest in my new tomb.

Mary was almost hysterical. "I anointed him for burial ahead of time . . . but I have nothing to anoint him with now!"

"There isn't time, anyway," I rebuked her. "It's almost sunset, and the start of the Sabbath. We hardly have time to close the tomb."

But, try as we might, Nicodemus and I couldn't roll the stone over the opening. (That's what comes of always insisting on the best quality everything. Any two men can easily roll an *ordinary* tombstone, but mine was so heavy it would have taken a half-dozen!)

In fact, it did. Just at dusk, a detail of six Roman soldiers arrived at my garden. Pilate had sent them to guard the tomb. They inspected the grave and the body wrapped in its shroud, and then they heaved and grunted and groaned—if it hadn't been so sad, it would have been really comical!—until they got the stone rolled into place. Then, as if to make things doubly secure, they sealed the rock to the tomb with pitch . . . and mounted their 'round-the-clock guard.

Mary and the other women had long since left . . . vowing that they would wait through the Sabbath . . . then buy some embalming herbs . . . and be back at dawn on the first day of the week to minister properly to the body of their dead lord.

I observe the Sabbath very strictly . . . or I would have gone out to Bethany to tell them that I had a whole storeroom of myrrh and aloes—that's my business, after all—so they needn't *buy* any, but that they . . . or we . . . wouldn't be able to roll back the stone to get into the tomb anyway.

I confess that I slept late this morning. I really haven't been emotionally involved in all this . . . except for Mary's sake . . . until today. My manservant finally woke me to tell me that Mary had been and gone . . . that the Roman guard had run off in a panic . . . that the stone at the tomb had been moved a good six feet away . . . and that the grave was empty.

It was . . . and is . . . almost. Only the grave clothes are there . . . the length of linen I bought . . . and the head covering I made . . . lying just as we left them . . . wrapped round a non-existent body . . . collapsed, sort of . . . almost deflated-looking . . . as though the body had decomposed to dust in a day . . . instead of a century . . . completely undisturbed.[15]

Mary came back briefly, around noon, to tell me what she knew about it. She says she saw and spoke to the Risen Lord—out in my garden[16]—and I believe her. She was radiant . . . as I've never seen her before; serene . . . as though she were living in another world; lovely . . . as if she could change the world simply by smiling on it.

She told me how she had worried, all the way over from Bethany: who would roll away the stone?—since Nicodemus wouldn't be there to help me. (Little did she know!)

"The Lord rolled away the stone, Joseph—not only from the tomb—but also from my heart.

"I've always secretly doubted him, Joseph—doubted that he would die, as he said he must—doubted even more that he could rise from the dead, as he said he would.

"But that stone of doubt is rolled away, Joseph. I'm free: free to trust him . . . free to love him . . . free to live for him . . . free to let him live through me.

"Some of the others don't believe it yet, Joseph. I've got to

15. John 20:6-8.
16. John 20:11 ff.

go to them . . . to tell them I saw him . . . to convince them he's risen . . . to roll away their stones of doubt . . . to set them free to live, too!"

And she was gone again.

"Some of the others don't believe it . . ." I can imagine!

I wonder if I believe it? Was he really dead? Yes—I handled the stiff, cold body.

Who rolled away the stone? No earthly power that I can imagine or find any trace of—the Governor has been exhausting his men and mine in *that* search.

Did the disciples steal the body? That's the story Pilate and the chief priests are already putting out by way of damage control. But the grave-clothes were intact . . . and undisturbed.[17]

What *difference* does it make? Well, Mary is a new person . . . a profoundly new person. She's alive—like she says Jesus is. She has a vitality, and a glow, and a spirit I've never known . . .

. . . but I'd *like* to know—and *have*—for myself. She says a stone has been rolled away from her heart . . . a stone of doubt and fear . . . and that she feels free . . . free to trust . . . free to love . . . free to live.

I'm beginning to think that's what this "resurrection" business is all about: a stone rolled away at the very heart of everything.

Could I believe that? Do I already?

Lord, I *do* believe . . . *sort of*: help my unbelief![18]

---

17. Matthew 28:11-15.

18. A reference to the plea of the hapless father of the boy afflicted with seizures in Mark 9:24; see also Matthew 9:14-29 and Luke 9:37-43a.

— XIII —

JOSEPH BAR-SABBAS
("JUSTUS" — PART ONE)

BACKGROUND COMMENTARY

IN THE WINTER OF 1992, I began looking for a character
with whom to create another Easter soliloquy. Joseph of
Arimathea had been in my repertoire for almost 15 years
by then—but his garden continued to fascinate me as a setting
for yet another re-telling of the resurrection story. I began to
think about the possibilities inherent in the gardener, with
whom Mary Magdalene might have had at least a passing ac-
quaintance; and I began to research New Testament names to
give to this emerging identity.

At the same time, I was already looking ahead to the tran-
sition time between spring and summer, traditionally marked
in the First Presbyterian Church of Deerfield on Pentecost Sunday, for which I also wanted to present a soliloquy sermon that
year. One day, as I was reading in the first chapter of the Book
of the Acts of the Apostles, I began to speculate about the two
men nominated to take the place of Judas Iscariot among the
Twelve as "witnesses with us to the resurrection."[1] Here were
two otherwise unknown and unidentified individuals—yet
both, apparently, known to the Lord's followers somehow as
"witnesses" to the resurrection—one of whom was elected by
the casting of lots, the other defeated, as it were—and neither
of them ever heard of again!

In another of my soliloquies,[2] I make a point of the coinci-

1. Acts 1:21-26.
2. CHAPTER XVII, "Agent of Death/Angel of Life."

dence of the man offered by Pontius Pilate as an alternate to Jesus to be freed at the Passover—Barabbas (in Aramaic bar-Abbas)—having the same given name as our Lord—"Jesus." Because of that unconnected bit of trivia, somehow, the surname of one of the apostle candidates—"bar-Sabbas"—caught my attention and literally fired my imagination. I did a little etymological research on the Aramaic word *sabbas* and its possible derivation from the Hebrew root for "Sabbath." I already knew that *bar* meant "son of" and could be interpreted (as I had already done in my soliloquy on Barabbas) as implying illegitimacy. The nickname "Justus" just seemed right for a gardener—and allowed me a bit of humor with the nonsensical word play on the proverbial wheels of justice grinding so slowly! One day, it was just as though the about-to-be-speaker of my soliloquy stood up and introduced himself!

As much as possible, the whole of this message is grounded in the Gospel of John: John the Baptist's testimony on the occasion of Jesus' baptism;[3] Nicodemus' visit to Jesus by night;[4] the request to Pilate to release Jesus' body for burial;[5] and the resurrection story with Mary Magdalene as the first person to encounter the Risen Lord.[6] But, as is the case in most of my soliloquies, there are elements drawn from the Synoptic Gospels as well: the suggestion that Joseph of Arimathea was a wealthy perfume merchant hints at the story lines in the monologues in CHAPTERS VII and XII, with their references to the anointing of Jesus;[7] the concern of Pilate and the chief priests to guard against a staged "resurrection" after the burial of Jesus;[8] and the account of the Ascension at the end of Luke segueing into the

3. John 1:29-34.
4. John 3:1ff.
5. John 19:38-42.
6. John 20:11ff.
7. Matthew 26:6-13, Mark 14:3-9.
8. Matthew 27:62-66.

first chapter of Acts;[9] are the three most obvious non-Johannine elements.

In essence, this sermon is simply an imaginative retelling of the Easter story, which I have always believed is just about the most powerful thing a preacher can do before an Easter Sunday multitude. But for the committed faithful there is Justus' theologically thought-provoking suggestion that perhaps we are often mistaken about Jesus: "putting him into our categories . . . squeezing him into our expectations . . . limiting him to our needs." And for the "C&E" crowd, there is the intriguing redefinition of the Easter miracle as "the power of God . . . let loose in the world in a way that none of us expected . . . that few of us are ready for . . . that maybe even fewer of us even want." And for everyone there's the question that hangs in the air at the end: "If it is true, what a difference it will make—in my life—and in yours—won't it?"

As often as I have presented this soliloquy, I have wondered whether I would be challenged—or even rebuked—for having brazenly appropriated words that John's Gospel attributes to Jesus, and giving them to Justus. But somehow the questions "Woman, why are you weeping? Whom are you looking for?"[10] don't sound quite *right* as the first utterance of the Risen Lord— but *do* sound *exactly right* as the innocent and insensitive queries of a gardener Mary could quite reasonably have suspected of having moved the Lord's body during the time the tomb was unattended. And that dialogue sets Justus up to make the powerful faith assertions that "it was *not* I who spoke her name. It was *not* I she saw when she looked through eyes of faith. It was *not* I who spoke of ascending to God the Father. It was *not* I

---

9. Luke 24:50-53 and Acts 1:6ff.
10. John 20:15.

whose presence was like the dawning of a new day, the opening of a new world, the inaugural of a new kingdom of peace and joy and love."

* * * * *

MISTAKEN IDENTITY

Jesus said to her,
"Woman, why are you weeping? Whom are you looking for?"
Supposing him to be the gardener, she said to him:
"Sir, if you have carried him away, tell me where you have laid him,
and I will take him away."
Jesus said to her, "Mary!"

(JOHN 20:15-16)

Someone once said, "Everybody's famous for fifteen minutes."

Well, my fame lasted maybe fifteen seconds—but it was a moment I've always treasured—a moment I'll never forget.

My name is Joseph bar-Sabbas . . . but most folks call me "Justus." My names are sort of a joke—a cruel joke, actually—but I don't let it bother me much—at least not any more.

You see I was born without a father, if you know what I mean. Boys born to unwed mothers who are known to be tramps are usually call "bar-Abbas"—which means literally "son of a father . . . any father." But my mother was the daughter of a fine family—a girl with too much idle time and too little worthwhile to do. She was seduced by an irresponsible young man of similar birth and background—who was banished from Jerusalem for his sin—and I was born "bar-Sabbas" . . . "son of the Sabbath" . . . the product of too much leisure and too little character.

I grew up in my mother's family home: the unwanted child who had to be provided for, but could never become the son and heir my grandfather so desperately wanted. My mother, who never married, spoiled me, pampered me, indulged me, ruined me for any useful, productive life. In adolescence, fat and lazy, I was nicknamed "Justus" because, like the wheels of justice, I moved so slow!

My grandfather died when I was fifteen. My great-uncle inherited everything. He turned out to be a pompous, self-righteous old Pharisee who agreed to allow my mother and my grandmother to remain in his household only on the condition that I be thrown, literally, into the street. I had nowhere to go . . . no money . . . no family . . . suddenly no friends. I ended up on the doorstep of my namesake, my father's elder brother, Joseph, an immensely wealthy perfume merchant with estates in Arimathea and a mansion on the edge of Jerusalem overlooking the Damascus Gate.

Uncle Joseph felt compassion for me, and made a place for me in his household, on the understanding that I would earn my keep. He put me to work as an apprentice gardener—a job I learned to love so much I've kept at it ever since. Now I'm the head gardener here at Joseph's house in Jerusalem . . . and, more than that, I've become my uncle's friend and confidante.

Uncle Joseph has a surprising... and dangerous... and well-kept secret—or he did, until the past couple of days. About three years ago, he was greatly impressed by the preaching and prophetic ministry of a man who came to be known as John the Baptist. We used to go out into the desert, on the pretext of traveling down to Arimathea, but actually in order to hear John's powerful messages about repentance and faithfulness and the coming of the Messiah.

One day, when John was baptizing converts in the River Jordan, my uncle, who is a very dignified, aristocratic, private person, felt so moved by the Baptist's call to repentance that, to my complete amazement, he went down into the water with the many others. I watched from the river bank as John moved slowly through the water, baptizing first one, then another, coming ever closer to my uncle. When Joseph was next but one, John stopped, as though struck by a vision, and began to prophesy about the man standing before him in the water:

> *Here is the Lamb of God who takes away the sin of the world!... this is the Son of God.*[11]

Uncle Joseph never was baptized that day... but from then on, he became a secret follower of Jesus of Nazareth, the Son of God, the one we believe to be the Messiah. Whenever he could, he would arrange to be wherever Jesus was preaching and teaching. Sometimes I would accompany him; sometimes I would go to be with Jesus and the Twelve in his place. From the beginning, there has been opposition to Jesus' ministry—even more so than to John's—so Uncle Joseph, and his friend, Nicodemus,[12] another secret believer, have had to be very, very careful:

11. John 1:29-34.
12. John 7:50-52.

they're members of the Sanhedrin—powerful and influential men in their own right—but, until now, they have always believed that they could do Jesus more good by distancing themselves from the political side of his coming Kingdom.

That all changed this past week. Everything went wrong at once. Jesus was betrayed by one of the Twelve . . . got arrested Thursday night by the henchmen of the High Priest . . . appeared before Pontius Pilate early Friday morning . . . and was sentenced to death by crucifixion and summarily executed at Calvary . . . all before Uncle Joseph and Nicodemus could exert their influence to put a stop to any of it.

In the end, the most the two men could do was to go to Pilate and ask permission to take Jesus' body away from Calvary for burial . . . which they did.[13] I was tasked with preparing the new family tomb to receive its first corpse. What a sad duty! I had come to know Jesus so well; and, in my own slow-witted and understated way, had begun to believe that he *was* the promised Messiah, the One who would come in the Name of the Lord to save us from our sins. How could it have ended like this?

Even with Jesus dead and about to be buried, the chief priests and the Pharisees were still nervous. They remembered, apparently far more clearly than did Jesus' followers, the Master's mystifying teaching that, on the third day, he would rise from the dead.[14] So they persuaded Pilate to assign an armed guard to the gravesite. Their soldiers, in turn, bullied me and my men into sealing the mouth of the tomb-cave with thick black pitch before we rolled the heavy stone back into place.

All for naught. Since yesterday was the Sabbath, and the

13. John 19:38-42.
14. Matthew 27:62-66.

first day of Passover, too, I didn't dare do a lick of work; so, at first light this morning, I slipped out into my beloved garden to try to put to rights some of the mess that had been made the night before last. I could hardly imagine what a campfire and a squad of mercenaries might have done to my rhododendrons and orange blossoms!

But what I found was a heap of ashes, still smoldering, but no sign of the soldiers. Looking around, I realized that the huge stone sealing the tomb had been rolled away—not altogether—but enough that someone could come or go with ease. How could that have happened?

Before I summoned up the courage to look inside, I heard footsteps approaching, and muffled voices. Terrified that it might be the soldiers, and that I might be held responsible for whatever had been done, I scurried into the bushes and hid.

It was two of the disciples—Simon Peter, I think, and maybe John—followed by Mary, who, it turned out, had already been there earlier that morning with some of the other women.[15] The disciples looked into the tomb, glanced around dumbfounded, talked a bit, and left before I could disentangle myself from the shrubbery in which I had been hiding.

Mary, weeping bitterly, was left alone in the garden . . . although perhaps not all alone, for I was sure I heard her speaking to someone else, or maybe just to herself: "They have taken away my Lord, and I do not know where they have laid him."[16]

Not wanting to startle her, but anxious to let her know that she was not alone, I stepped out of the shrubbery and asked softly, "Why are you weeping? Whom are you looking for?"[17]

She turned, and began to implore me, "Sir, if you have car-

---

15. John 20:1-18.
16. John 20:13.
17. John 20:15.

ried him away, tell me where you have laid him, and I will take him away."[18]

I opened my mouth to reply, when a voice not my own said simply, "Mary!"[19]

I *knew* it was Jesus: not *how*, or *where*, or *why* . . . just *that* it was the Master . . . and that the intensity and intimacy of his presence there was not for me, but for her, and for her alone. I slipped back into the shrubbery, closed my eyes and opened my heart, and knew that it was true: Jesus *had* risen from the dead on the third day, just as he had foretold!

When she tells the others, some will probably say that Mary was imagining things . . . or that it was I she saw and spoke to . . . or that the grief and pain of the past few days had finally become too much for her.[20]

I know better: it *was* I she saw—for a moment at least—but it was *not* I who spoke her name. It was *not* I she saw when she looked through eyes of faith. It was *not* I who spoke of ascending to God the Father. It was *not* I whose presence was like the dawning of a new day, the opening of a new world, the inaugural of a new kingdom of peace and joy and love.

I think Mary is the first of us to have seen Jesus as he really is: not just a son of man, but the Son of God. We've all been mistaken about him: putting him into our categories . . . squeezing him into our expectations . . . limiting him to our needs. More than a prophet . . . much more than a rabbi . . . certainly much, much more than a messianic political deliverer: he's a miracle . . . a living witness to the victory of life over death, of right over wrong, of love over hate; he's a savior . . . a Lord . . . a promise forevermore.

18. Ibid.
19. John 20:16.
20. Luke 24:11 and Mark 16:11.

I wonder what will happen when I tell Uncle Joseph? He has been praying for this very thing to occur. Will he be able to believe that such a wonder has actually been wrought out of his tomb? Will *I* be able to accept that such a miracle has come to pass in my garden . . . almost before my eyes?

And what *difference* will it make? I tremble to think that the Word of God has come so very close to my life . . . that the love of God has burst out of the tomb in which I helped bury it . . . that the power of God has been let loose in the world in a way that none of us expected . . . that few of us are ready for . . . that maybe even fewer of us even *want*.

It's almost too much to understand . . . to accept . . . to believe. Yet . . . if it *is* true, what a difference it will make—in my life—and in yours—won't it?

— XIV —

THOMAS

BACKGROUND COMMENTARY

A S A BOY GROWING up in an exurban area outside Windsor, Ontario, I attended the only elementary school within reasonable walking distance, a Roman Catholic parochial institution staffed by Sisters of the Holy Names of Jesus and Mary. For most of my six years there, I was the only Protestant student in the school, and my parents made it plain to the Sister Principal that I was not to be proselytized in any way—a stipulation the nuns scrupulously respected.

Or so I thought until, one mind-wandering afternoon in a New Testament Greek class at Princeton Theological Seminary, I was reminiscing for no good reason at all about the pride and joy with which I had once participated in a post-Easter school pageant organized by the good sisters—who cast me, I realized with belated amusement, as "Doubting Thomas!"

In today's world, it is hermeneutically preferred to refer to Thomas as "confessing" rather than "doubting." But when I imagined my way through the preparation of this soliloquy, I was wrestling with doubts of my own. My wife had been gravely ill, in fact near death, and my own faith resources were worn dangerously thin. One of the elders in the Deerfield congregation, a self-made millionaire with a powerfully entrepreneurial outlook on life, was challenging my weekly interpretations of Scripture with questions about the "reality" of various Gospel events, in particular the Johannine account of Jesus' raising Lazarus from the grave,[1] and what that story had to say to his own unresolved grief work following the death of his father a few months before.

At that time in my ministry, the thrust of Jesus' appearance to Thomas, after previously appearing to the other disciples while Thomas was not present, had always seemed to be more a matter of rebuking his follower's stubborn faithlessness than of eliciting his breathless faith confession. And the preaching point for my congregants would surely have been the blessed-ness pronounced upon those "who have not seen and yet have come to believe,"[2] with particular reference to the resurrection of our Lord and the prospect of life beyond death with Him and in Him.

So Thomas "the realist" was becoming more and more real for me in the Lenten season of 1997 as I plodded through an ill-advised sermon series based on a small study book of readings titled "Listening for God." I realized that I wanted—and needed—to "listen for God" in the creative context of writing a new soliloquy for Easter that would speak to, and for, me, as much as to my parishioners, in a more powerful and persuasive way than I felt had been happening that winter.

Since everything I could discern about the personality and point of view of the disciple Thomas came from material provided by the Fourth Evangelist, it seemed natural to restrict my other Scriptural references pretty much to the Gospel of John. Since it had long been my custom to read the first verses of John 14 ("Do not let your hearts be troubled . . .") at funerals and memorial services, of which we had had an inordinate number that

---

1. John 11:1-44.
2. John 20:29.

156 William R. Russell

winter, I particularly wanted to explore Thomas' outburst "Lord, we do not know where you are going. How can we know the way?" and Jesus' enigmatic reply, "I am the way, and the truth, and the life."

The insight into the significance of *risk*—and the notion that it is *the risk factor* that differentiates true *faith* from mere *belief*—came out of my conversations with my entrepreneurial friend. It was he who helped me to comprehend that to believe without seeing, whether in business or in religion or in any other aspect of life, is to *risk everything*—Kierkegaard's proverbial "leap of faith!" Making that point to an Easter Sunday congregation proved more powerful and persuasive than I could ever have imagined when I started to explore experiencing Jesus from the "realistic" point of view of a doubter turned confessor. Men generally, and businessmen in particular, have responded to this one sermon soliloquy paragraph more frequently, and more fervently, than to almost anything else I have ever written or presented.

* * * * *

BELIEVING WITHOUT SEEING

Then Jesus said to Thomas,
"Put your finger here and see my hands.
Reach out your hand and put it in my side.
Do not doubt but believe."
Thomas answered him,
"My Lord and my God!"
(JOHN 20:27-28)

I didn't believe it!

They said they had seen the Lord—risen from the dead—the nail-holes still showing in his hands—the spear's gash still gaping in his side.

I didn't believe it!

They claimed that Jesus had appeared to them—earlier that evening—after they had locked themselves up in the house for fear of the authorities, and I had gone out for a walk because I couldn't stand being cooped up any longer . . . just waiting . . . doing nothing! They insisted that Jesus had blessed them with a 'peace that surpasses understanding', and had "sent"

---

3. Philippians 4:7.

them—they know not where—"as (they said he said) the Father had sent him."[4]

I didn't believe it happened!

When I got back from my walk, they were all excited—almost hysterical—just like the women who had gone to the Garden Tomb to embalm the Lord's body and had come away convinced that Jesus had been raised from the dead—so convinced that they had persuaded Simon Peter and John to go and have a look—and then they were saying they "saw and believed" it, too! I just couldn't take it any more. I told them: "Unless I see the mark of the nails in his hands, and put my finger in the mark of the nails and my hand in his side, I will not believe."[5]

I still don't believe I could have made such a fool of myself!

I don't think of myself as a "doubter"—just a "realist." Like when the Master's dearest friend, Lazarus, died ... and Jesus determined to go back across the Jordan River to Bethany to comfort Mary and Martha.[6] We were in Trans-Jordan because things had gotten a little out of hand in Jerusalem during Hanukkah, and some Jewish hot-heads had tried to stone Jesus because he would neither admit nor deny that he was the Messiah.[7] The other disciples tried to talk the Lord out of going back into Judea—but I knew that wouldn't work: Jesus wouldn't stay hidden in Trans-Jordan very much longer in any case.

I also knew how dangerous things really were over in Judea ... and I thought that we might as well face up to the fact that death was as likely an end to what we were about as any other. "Let's go," I rallied the rest of the twelve, "that we may die with him."[8] So we did.

And the result wasn't *death*, but *life*. The Master raised

4. John 20:21.
5. John 20:25.
6. John 11:1-44.
7. John 10:22-42.
8. John 11:16.

Lazarus from the grave . . . and spoke about being "the resurrection and the life" in words that I thought I would never forget.

> *Those who believe in me,* (he said) *even though they die, will live, and everyone who lives and believes in me will never die.*[9]

Clearly, *that* promise went right out of my head when Jesus himself was put to death.

If I'm a realist, I guess I'm a pretty thick-headed one. I like everything simple and straightforward, clear and concise, nice and neat. So I got kind of impatient with the Master the other night during the Passover Seder when he started talking about going to "his father's house . . . to prepare a place for us."[10] Now I know as well as anyone that Joseph, the carpenter of Nazareth, is dead long since: so I supposed Jesus must be talking about his *heavenly* Father. But no sooner had I figured *that* out than the Master said:

> *If I go and prepare a place for you, I will come again and will take you to myself, so that where I am, there you may be also. And you know the way to the place where I am going.*[11]

Well, I *didn't* know where he was going—or where he wanted us to go either—so I said so:

> *Lord, we do **not** know where you are going. How can we know the way?*[12]

9. John 11:25-26.
10. John 14:1-4.
11. John 14:3-4.
12. John 14:5.

I am the way, (he explained) *and the truth, and the life.*[13]

Those were the last words Jesus ever spoke directly to me—at least until today—and they have haunted me through the horrors of this past week. I have been with Jesus from the start . . . and I have always felt as though we were really close (so close, in fact, that the disciples nicknamed me "the twin"[14] because I actually look so much like Jesus, and, with this Galilean accent, sound so much like him). But I have always thought of him just as a *teacher*—a "rabbi"—never as a *savior*—a "messiah"—in whose *person,* rather than in whose lessons, would be "the way, and the truth and the life."

That night in the Garden of Gethsemane . . . then the next morning at Pilate's court in the Antonia Fortress . . . then later during the crucifixion at Calvary . . . and later still when they buried him in the Arimathean's garden tomb . . . I kept wondering *how*—or *whether*—I had gotten it all so wrong.

I thought that Jesus was going to set everything right in black and white . . . that life was going to be simple . . . and faith was going to be straightforward . . . and morality was going to be strictly by the book . . . and hope was going to be a sure thing. But nothing has turned out the way I thought.

Jesus appeared to the disciples again today—again, somehow, through locked doors and shuttered windows—but, this time, I was in the house with them.[15] "Peace be with you," he said, as before. Then he said to me,

---

13. John 14:6.

14. John 11:16, 20:24, and 21:2. This "twin" identifier is unique to John's Gospel, as are each of the Gospel incidents in which Thomas is mentioned, other than the listings of the disciples. He was a disciple with whom the author of John was clearly fascinated.

15. John 20:26-29.

Put your finger here and see my hands. Reach out
your hand and put it in my side. Do not doubt but
believe.

I was so ashamed. How could I have *doubted* that he would
rise from the dead as he had promised? . . . as he had already
shown us he had the power to do by raising Lazarus?

For a moment I was speechless. I dropped to my knees before my Lord and my Savior—risen—triumphant—offering
himself *to* me (now I began to understand!) as he had offered
himself *for* me on that cross. And I blurted out:

My Lord and my God!

I wish I could tell you that that was the end of it—but it
wasn't. Leaving me on my knees—amazed and ashamed and
convinced and convicted all at once—Jesus said to me,

Have you believed because you have seen me? Blessed
are those who have not seen and yet have come to be-
lieve.

Of course! It doesn't take any *faith* to believe something you
can *see*. "Seeing is believing." But faith only comes into it when
you have to *risk* believing—when you *can't* see—*can't* check
out—*can't* verify—what you're being asked to believe. *Risk*—
not *sight*—is what makes belief *faith*. And *faith* is what makes
the unknown way followable . . . and the unprovable truth
sure . . . and the uncertain future the narrow gate that leads to
life abundant and everlasting.

162   *William R. Russell*

I've been asking the wrong questions . . . expecting the wrong results . . . demanding the wrong guarantees. I didn't need to stick my finger into the nail-hole in my Lord's hand . . . nor thrust my hand into his wounded side . . . nor hear his heart-broken voice . . . nor see his wondering face . . . to *know*[16] in whom I believe . . . in whom I can trust . . . in whom I want to live. (I can't imagine how I could ever have said such a stupid and silly thing!)

My Lord *loves* me—enough to die for me. My Lord *wants* me—enough to live for me. My Lord *cares* about me—enough to walk with me through every valley of the shadow this side of the grave . . . and into the brightness of God's glory on the other side . . . without ever once pretending there won't be valleys, and shadows, and a grave . . . and without ever once promising anything more than his presence and his power to see me through.

I still consider myself a "realist"—but this is a whole new kind of "reality" to get used to—and, without a doubt, it's going to take some getting used to. But, whenever I start to slip back into my old ways of thinking and acting and wanting to *see* and *not* wanting to *risk*, I'm going to remember Jesus standing there in risen splendor offering me his pierced hands and his torn side to do with as I would—challenging me . . . daring me . . . inviting me: "Make up your mind; don't be a doubter. Believe!"[17]

And I hope that I never forget how it felt to fall to my knees and say what I believe: "My Lord and my God!"

16. 2 Timothy 1:12.

17. John 20:27b as rendered in powerfully contemporary language by Eugene H. Peterson in *The Message*.

— XV —

ALPHAEUS
(PART TWO)

BACKGROUND COMMENTARY

THIS MONOLOGUE BEGAN as a companion piece to the post-Christmas soliloquy in the voice of Alphaeus, the imagined owner of the inn at Bethlehem in which there was "no room" for Mary and Joseph that first Christmas.[1] It was intended for presentation on the Sunday after Easter, in fulfillment of my pledge to myself to be in my own Millburn pulpit on that "low" Sunday.

But Alphaeus took on a life of his own, particularly as I wrestled withy the idea of his being that intriguing "man carrying a jar of water" introduced in Mark's and Luke's Gospels as the go-between signal for which Peter and John were to look in their task of making arrangements for Jesus and his disciples to eat the first Seder of Passover that fateful year.[2] That he should be a witness to the "Last Supper," and then to the Crucifixion, and finally to the Ascension of the Lord—and therein to reconnect with his long-lost wife and youngest child—seemed almost self-evident as I worked out the denouement to the Gospel identity of the ever-so-briefly mentioned disciple "James the son of Alphaeus."[3]

I confess that I was tempted—briefly!—to try to work in some reference to Mark's mention of the calling of "Levi, son of Alphaeus" and the telling account of the dinner during which Jesus spoke the unforgettable words, "Those who are well have

---

1. See CHAPTER IV, "If Only I Had Known ..."
2. Mark 14:12-16 and Luke 22:7-13.
3. Mentioned four times in the Synoptic listings of the Twelve: Matthew 10:3, Mark 3:18, Luke 6:15, and Acts 1:3.

no need of a physician, but those who are sick; I have come to call not the righteous but sinners."[4] But as I pondered the Gospel of Matthew's identification[5] of the same man as "Matthew"—with no specific paternal reference—and the Gospel of Luke's account[6] of the same events happening to a man identified as "Levi"—again, with no mention of parentage—I realized that I was facing a scriptural inconsistency far too complicated for the storyline on which I had been working. It was almost as though Alphaeus was telling me, "Don't go there!"

The same was true when I tried to reconcile the Gospel of John's identification of one of the Marys at the crucifixion as "the wife of Clopas."[7] The whole subject of the identities of the women present at the crucifixion is a difficult and contentious one. My "solution" might have been to reveal that, after so many years apart, Alphaeus' wife had remarried. But that additional sadness to the story line would have had to be the subject of yet another soliloquy—one to which Alphaeus seemed to say, "Don't go there either!"

It goes without saying, of course, that much of Alphaeus' sad story comes out of my own imagination, prompted here and there by bits of old traditions about the identities and fates of the lesser-known disciples and apostles. But the fictionalization of it all also allowed me to incorporate elements of the Johannine chronology of our Lord's last days on earth into the Synoptic time-line, especially the Maundy Thursday story of the foot-washing of the disciples.

The preaching point in this message turned out to be a statement of "realized eschatology" that surprised even me

---

4. Mark 2:13-17. Cf. Matthew 9:9-13 and Luke 5:27-32.
5. Matthew 9:9-13.
6. Luke 9:9-13.
7. John 19:25.

when Alphaeus first uttered it. His struggle to comprehend the impact of the Lord's resurrection and his promise of "life everlasting" upon the here-and-now of our everyday lives came out with a definition my congregations have come to cherish: "forgiveness of a life's worth of sins . . . and victory over old habits and real weaknesses . . . and reconciliation with those you love and have lost awhile . . . and renewal within yourself of hope, and confidence, and faith, and life itself."

Another surprise for me was the way Alphaeus' soliloquy–become–monologue unfolded its own story line, and lodged itself later in the church year calendar than I had intended. So, instead of on the Sunday after Easter, I first introduced Alphaeus to my Millburn congregation on the Sunday after Ascension Thursday in 1969. In congregations since, his message has become a powerful Communion meditation for whenever the Sacrament of the Lord's Supper was celebrated in the post-Easter, post-Ascension season. What I actually did for "something special" for my congregation on that Sunday after Easter of the first year of my Millburn ministry I can no longer remember!

* * * * *

In the Upper Room ... Again!

Now it was Mary Magdalene and Joanna
and Mary the mother of James and the other women with them
who told this to the disciples;
but these words seemed to them an idle tale,
and they did not believe them.

(LUKE 24:10-11)

You don't remember me, do you? . . . no, you couldn't possibly! It was a long time ago . . . and I was younger then, and better looking, and more prosperous, than now.

My name is Alphaeus . . . and when last we met, I still ran the inn in Bethlehem. My wife and children had just escaped from Herod's soldiers . . . right after our baby, James, was born so sickly—well, no matter, it was a long time ago.

Now I live here, in Jerusalem, in this big fancy house. Ha! . . . who am I kidding? . . . I live out back in the servants' quarters—and I'm grateful to be there. A year ago I was literally in the gutter: that's where the son of the master and mistress

found me—a fine boy named John Mark.[8] He brought me
home and sobered me up and persuaded his folks to give me a
job helping out in the kitchen.

   I've never told them my story, and they've never asked. Actually, there's not much to tell, My wife and children never came
back to Bethlehem after Herod's soldiers slaughtered all the boy
babies in town; and, truth to tell, I hadn't much heart for the
place, either![9]

   When there was no word from Mary—that's my wife—
after a year, I gave up the inn and went off looking for them. I
longed for Mary, and I missed the older children, Joses[10] and
Miriam. But, most of all, I wondered about little James, who
had been born so gravely ill, and was so clearly near death when
we laid him in the manger to fool the Roman soldiers . . . and, I
like to think, perhaps saved that other baby—the one I suspect
the soldiers were actually looking for—the one born in our stable around that same time because I had told his parents there
was no room for them at my inn. Remember, I described to you
once before, how the soldiers hadn't bothered to kill our son—

---

   8. See Acts 12:12. There is a long-standing tradition that the house to
which Peter fled after his prison escape was the same one in which the disciples hid after the crucifixion, and to which they returned after the ascension of the Lord. By inference, I have made it the same house in which Jesus
had previously made arrangements for his "last supper" with his Twelve. Was
this "John Mark" the same person mentioned in Acts 12:25 and 15:37 and
39 as a conflict-causing companion to Paul and Barnabas, let alone the
"cousin" of Barnabas mentioned in Colossians 4:10, the "fellow worker"
named in Philemon 1:24, or the "son" claimed by Peter in I Peter 5:13?
Could he have been the source of the oral tradition that eventually became
transcribed into the Gospel of Mark? All of these possibilities intrigue me
as the basis for another soliloquy—one I have yet to create!

   9. Matthew 2:16ff.

   10. See Mark 15:40 and 47 where a man with this name appears as a
brother to "James" and as a son of "Mary," There is some identity confusion
in Mark's Gospel, though, since in 6:3 the evangelist appears to identify Joses
as among the several siblings of Jesus himself!

because he was half-dead anyway—and how, after they tumbled him back into that manger and left, James started getting better.

At first, I really felt that a miracle had taken place. I really believed—and hoped—that that *other* baby would become what everyone was expecting: the Messiah of Israel! But the miracle turned into a nightmare ... the hope, a pipe dream ... the salvation, a sick joke. I never could find Mary and the children, and, eventually, I gave up looking. I did odd jobs ... and scrounged ... and begged ... and drifted. I found solace when and where I could—sometimes, with a woman; more often, with a bottle—until the days and weeks and months and years became a blur of emptiness ... and I ended up here, under the care of John Mark.

His parents are pretty rich ... and keep a lot of servants to run this big house. My job is the water: every day I go back and forth to the local well with a big jar, and fill up the cisterns in the kitchen and the wash basins around the house. Most households have women doing this work, and I look pretty silly out in the street with that water jar on my head—the only man among all those women—but the master says I'm old and shaky, and it's the only work I'm fit to do.

Actually, the fact that I stand out among the women at the well is why John Mark used me as the signal to guide those two men here just before Passover.[11] It turns out that John Mark was a secret follower of a famous rabbi from Galilee, and had offered him and his disciples the use of our upper room for their Passover Seders. That caused an awful row between John Mark and his parents: they knew that the Sanhedrin opposed the

11. Mark 14:12ff. and Luke 22:10ff.—a detail obviously well known in the Synoptic traditions. I have always wondered why the writer of Matthew chose not to include it in his pre-Passion narrative.

rabbi's teachings . . . and they thought him just an itinerant
street corner rabble-rouser anyhow . . . but they finally agreed
to let John Mark have his way on the condition that none of the
servants would be allowed to have anything to do with the
preparation or the serving of the feast.

I felt pretty bad about that. Normally, I would have been
the one assigned to wash the feet of our guests as they reclined
around the table . . . but I was forbidden . . . and none of the disciples would do it for the others . . . so the rabbi finally got up
and washed their feet himself.[12]

I watched it all from the kitchen door, and had the uncanny
feeling that I had seen that rabbi somewhere before . . . or at
least that he *looked* like someone I had seen before. There was
another man at the table—way down at the far end—who
looked familiar, too. He was very short, and thin, and pale, but
in the flickering lamplight, he looked uncannily like *me* . . . or
like I looked when I was a lot younger![13]

After supper, and that strange ceremony of sharing the
bread and wine, they all went out to the Mount of Olives; and—
well, I guess you've heard about it—the rabbi was arrested in
the Garden of Gethsemane . . . and his disciples all ran
away . . . and the next morning he was tried before the High
Priest, and then before the Governor, and then was sentenced
to death.

The household here was in an uproar, I can tell you! There
was so much worry and confusion that I was able to slip away
unnoticed to see the crucifixion. It was absolutely gruesome! At

---

12. See John 13:3ff. Although the Gospel of John's timeline and dating
for the Holy Week events differ significantly from the Synoptic traditions,
I felt that this "Maundy Thursday" story fit well into Alphaeus' recounting
of the "Last Supper" experience.

13. In the KJV, Mark 15:40 identifies James as "the Less(er)" rather than
"the younger"

one point, as he was dying, the rabbi spoke to one of the women at the foot of the cross, and called her "mother."[14] I looked, and recognized her right off: even after thirty-some years, she was definitely the woman who had given birth to that wondrous baby in our old stable out back of the inn in Bethlehem! And right beside her, weeping as though her heart would break, was my own Mary, the mother of my children![15]

I simply froze: so many wild, impossible, wonderful, confused thoughts came to my mind. Obviously my wife had somehow met, and become friends with, the mother of the rabbi, Jesus; and, no doubt, that frail young man at the far end of the table the night before must have been my own younger son, James.[16] Even as I tried to sort it all out, the rabbi died. From out of the crowd, John Mark appeared beside the women, and took them away. I followed . . . and eventually he brought them back here.

All through that night, the others kept coming back, too, until the upper room was full of the rabbi's followers. They were all grief-stricken . . . and terrified . . . and seemed to be expecting something more to happen: but they just wanted to be alone together . . . and so we servants weren't allowed upstairs. I was about frantic: my wife and son, whom I hadn't seen in more than thirty years, under the same roof—and I couldn't go near them!

14. John 19:26-7.

15. See Matthew 27:55 and Mark 15:40, from which I believed I derived sufficient justification to place Alphaeus' wife at the foot of the cross. Luke 23:49 refers generically to "the women who had followed [Jesus] from Galilee." John's Gospel (19:25) presented me with the challenge of the mention of "Mary, the wife of Clopas." The whole subject of the identities of the women present at the crucifixion is a difficult and contentious one. My "solution" might have been to reveal that, after so many years apart, Alphaeus' wife had remarried, but that additional sadness to the story line would have had to be the subject of yet another soliloquy—one to which I have never yet turned my attention.

16. Luke 6:15 and Acts 1:13.

Then I began to think maybe I *shouldn't* go near them. Look what I had become: a burned-out, empty old man . . . a derelict . . . a servant . . . a failure. They had griefs and burdens enough without having to deal with *me*!

On the morning after the Sabbath, some of the women, including my wife and the rabbi's mother, went out to the place where they had buried Jesus to do the proper ritual cleansing and embalming of the body.[17] Pretty soon they were back, with a hysterical story about his rising from the dead![18] A few of the men ran out then, and came back with the same story. That night, two of the disciples arrived from Emmaus very late, with news that Jesus had had supper with them there, and had shared the bread and wine in that special ceremonial way.[19]

A few days later, apparently, the risen Jesus appeared in this very house. I know, because one of the disciples, Thomas, a surly chap who never takes anything at face value, told me himself that he had *seen* "the Lord"—as everybody calls Him now— and could have put his fingers in the nail holes in the Lord's hands, if that's what it would take to make him believe.[20]

The impact of it all on everybody is what's unbelievable. John Mark is radiant . . . like a saint! His parents have turned round 180 degrees . . . and now welcome the "People of the Way" into their home . . . and have even become kinder and gentler and more considerate to the servants. The Lord's mother looks serene and beautiful . . . like a queen. My Mary seems years younger . . . so much the woman I remember that it almost breaks my heart. And James . . . James is taller, I swear . . . and

17. Mark 16:1 and Luke 24:10 both mention "Mary, the mother of James." Matthew 28:1 identifies "Mary Magdalene and *the other Mary*" as witnesses to the resurrection; in the Johannine story, Mary Magdalene is apparently alone.

18. Luke 24:10-1.

19. Luke 24:13ff.

20. John 20:26ff.

more robust ... and has a little color in his cheeks ... a second miracle, it really is!

Right now, they've all gone over to the Mount of Olives to be with the Lord before he "ascends to His Father," whatever that means[21]—and I've had some time to think. Actually, I feel like a new person, too—as though just being in the same house with the risen Lord and his followers has given me new strength, and new hope, and new courage, and new peace.

I feel as though I could make a fresh start, as old as I am! I'd like to go back to Bethlehem, and see if the old inn is still there, and try my hand at fixing it up and running it again. I don't think I'll ever go back to the bottle—I just don't need that kind of comfort any more.

I know that I've got up the courage, at last, to tell Mary ... and James ... who I am. Since the Lord rose, there is so much forgiveness around here, so much love among his followers, so much hope for the unknown future, that I feel sure my wife and son will forgive my past ... and understand my weakness ... and accept me as I am ... and help me rebuild a life together.

I can't figure out someone "rising from the dead"—and the idea of "everlasting life" doesn't make much sense to me. But I know what the Lord's being risen and alive has meant in this house ... and in the hearts of all these people ... and in my own personal experience. And if it means nothing more than forgiveness of a life's worth of sins ... and victory over old habits and real weaknesses ... and reconciliation with those you love and have lost awhile ... and renewal within yourself of hope, and confidence, and faith, and life itself—well, that's more than

21. John 20:17.

enough for me.

Here they come back.[22] I can hear them singing hymns out in the garden. I've got to go and make myself presentable to greet my wife ... and to meet my son. Pray for me—that things turn out the way I've said.

And I'll pray for you: that the Risen Lord may mean strength, and hope, and peace, and love, in your home ... and in your heart, too ...

22. Acts 1:12ff.

— XVI —

JOSEPH BAR-SABBAS

("JUSTUS" PART TWO)

BACKGROUND COMMENTARY

W HEN I HAPPENED upon the name and identity I would adopt for my Easter 1992 soliloquy,[1] I also found the protagonist for the Pentecost message I wanted to present that same year. "Joseph called Bar-sabbas, who was also known as Justus,"[2] seemed to fit the bill perfectly as both the gardener whom Mary Magdalene mistook for the risen Lord Jesus Christ and the "also-ran" who did not win the lot-casting election for an apostle to replace Judas Iscariot among the Twelve.[3]

Pentecost Sunday in the First Presbyterian Church of Deerfield, Illinois had by then become "a big deal." It marked the end of the Church School year and the beginning of the summer hiatus in Christian Education activities in general; so it was the day on which all the many and varied categories of Christian Education volunteers were recognized and honored in worship. It was celebrated as "the birthday of the Church" complete with a huge candle-lit cake and the children's shrill singing of "Happy Birthday!" And in 1992, it was the occasion for my introduction of a dramatic reading of selected verses from the second chapter of the Acts of the Apostles featuring many voices speaking many languages all at once.

Two separate and very different pastoral concerns converged in the imagining of this soliloquy. First, 1992 was prov-

1. See CHAPTER XIII, "Mistaken Identity."
2. Acts of the Apostles 1:23.
3. Acts of the Apostles 1:21-26.

ing to be a difficult year for many families in that congregation. Corporate "downsizing" had left a number of heads-of-households unemployed; new executive and professional positions commensurate with the stature and salary of the old jobs were few and far between; and hearts were as heavy as the mortgages and credit card payments a lot of families were barely managing to cover month by month.

The "wannabe" apostle, Justus, became the voice for the widespread feelings of disappointment, hurt, shock, worthlessness, discouragement, confusion, unhappiness—even suicide!—which I thought I might find it uncomfortable to address directly as my people's pastor, friend and neighbor, but which Justus could confess out loud in a way with which so many of my hearers might instantly identify. His celebration of the Lord Jesus as the *Someone* who kept him back from self-destruction, kept him sane, kept him "locked in a loving embrace from which [he] could neither escape nor want to" proved to be the most powerful sermon I could have preached to that congregation on that occasion.

My second pastoral concern at that time was the discomfort of many, not only in my congregation, but throughout the mainline North American denominations, with a rising tide of Pentecostalism and, in particular, *glossolalia* (speaking in tongues). I wanted to set that movement in a context that would accurately depict and define the Scriptural account of the apostles' amazing and perplexing feat of speaking "in other languages, as the Spirit gave them ability."[4] And I wanted to express the feelings of wholeness, happiness, healing and health that I believe are truly part of the experience of the gifts of the Holy

---

4. Acts 2:1-12.

Spirit even for those of us who resist the more ecstatic manifestations of that form of Christian spirituality. To have Justus say that he felt "inspired, encouraged, empowered, content, energized, optimistic, and eager to get on with whatever God's providence and Christ's lordship and the Holy Spirit's inspiration have in store . . ." was, as it turned out, an even more powerful preaching point for many of my hearers than the reassurances I mentioned earlier.

* * * * *

The also-ran

So they proposed two,
Joseph called Bar-sabbas, who was also known as Justus,
and Matthias . . .
And they cast lots for them,
and the lot fell on Matthias; and he was added to the eleven apostles.
(ACTS 1:23 AND 26)

I wanted it so badly, I could taste it: "apostle!"

To be an apostle of the living Lord—a witness to the resurrection of Jesus the Christ "in Jerusalem, in all Judea and Samaria, and to the ends of the earth"[5]—as the Lord himself had commanded the other eleven just before he was lifted up into the heavens, and a cloud took him out of our sight! What a calling! What a commission for a one-time gardener! What a chance for me to make something of a life that I have always thought was just about useless!

Perhaps you don't remember me. There's really no reason why you should. I'm Joseph Bar-Sabbas, although most people still call me Justus. We met, briefly, about a month ago, in the

5. Acts 1:7.

midst of the excitement about the Lord's resurrection from the
dead. I'm the head gardener for Joseph of Arimathea . . . and I
was there . . . and saw it all . . . and even had Mary Magdalene
mistake the Risen Lord for me!

Talk about excitement! It 's been nonstop since then! Jesus
kept appearing to the disciples . . . and to other believers . . . including myself . . . right here in Uncle Joseph's house, where the
eleven have been locked away in hiding for fear of the chief
priests and their soldiers.[6]

We've all been in such turmoil; yet the Lord always spoke
of "peace" . . . and of a commission to preach the "gospel of
peace" . . . and of a gift he called "Holy Spirit" that would em-
power us to go out into the world to proclaim God's love, God's
mercy, God's forgiveness, God's peace.

Then, just as suddenly and inexplicably as it began, it
ended . . . just over a week ago . . . at Bethany, of all places, where
it had sort of all started, with that "triumphal" procession into
Jerusalem at Passover. The Lord commanded the faithful to
gather there. He taught us again from the Scriptures . . . and
gave us a new understanding of his death and resurrection . . .
and challenged us to proclaim repentance, and forgiveness, and
life everlasting, in his name, to all nations . . . and lifted up his
hands to bless us as he loved to do . . . and, in that very moment,
was carried up, before our eyes, into heaven . . . disappearing in
the clouds even as we were worshiping him.[7]

We returned to Jerusalem with strangely mixed emotions:
grief in our loss of the one we loved more than life itself; joy at
the affirmation of our faith we experienced as Jesus was lifted
up into heaven; expectancy for the mysterious gift of Holy

6. John 20:19ff.
7. Luke 24:44ff.

Spirit promised by the Risen Christ; anxiety over the mounting anger and frustration being shown by the leaders of the Jews who could still not truly account for the disappearance of the corpse of their mortal enemy.

One day, to break the monotony of our waiting for we-knew-not-what, Simon Peter proposed to the whole group— there must have been about 120 of us in all by now—that we hold an election to replace Judas Iscariot and restore to twelve the inner core of disciples (whom we now began to call "apostles" because their period of learning from the Lord was over, and their commission to be witnesses to the resurrection was about to begin). Peter suggested that the criterion for eligibility to join the twelve should be that the person elected must have been a companion of the disciples from the very beginning, from the baptism of Jesus by John, even to the very end, to the ascension of the Lord into heaven.

When it came right down to it, there were only two of us who met Peter's eligibility requirement: Matthias and myself. I was sure that I would win! Matthias was a shoemaker, a shy man, devout but dreary, who could hardly bear witness to his wife, let alone to the whole world! I was only a gardener, I realized; but I was outgoing, and personable, and had actually been there in the garden when Jesus rose from the dead. No contest!

And that's just what happened: no contest. Before we voted, we prayed—that God would show us which one of the two should be chosen to have a place in this ministry of apostleship—and then someone suggested that, in the spirit of that prayer, we not mark ballots, but rather use the old-fashioned method of casting lots—like the once-sacred Urim and Thummim[8]—dark for Justus, light for Matthias—and the lots fell light, and Matthias became the apostle, rather than me.

I was so shocked! . . . so disappointed! . . . so hurt!

It would have been bad enough not to be chosen by the other eleven—that I could have lived with—but not to be chosen by God? *That* was almost unbearable. I put on a brave front (I had been doing that my whole miserable life!) . . . congratulated Matthias and wished him well in his new ministry . . . and fled to my beloved garden, where I wept bitterly until no more tears would come.

A week passed . . . and I was inconsolable. I felt so worthless . . . so unwanted . . . so unnecessary. It seemed as though every negative thought I had ever had about myself . . . my life . . . my worth . . . came surging back full force. I was so desperately unhappy that I even thought of doing away with myself—as poor confused Judas Iscariot had done.

But something—no, I realize now, some*one*—kept me back . . . kept me sane . . . kept me locked in a loving embrace from which I could neither escape nor want to. That something—that *Someone*—was my Lord Jesus, ascended into heaven where I would never see him again this side of the grave, yet somehow nearer to me than ever in my hurt and confusion and unhappiness.

Then, early this morning, there came the moment of promise for which everyone in our group has been waiting. We were in the house . . . at prayer . . . as we have been every Lord's Day since the Day of Resurrection . . . when the low murmur of our praying began to fade into a whispering wind . . . soft, at first . . . then more and more insistent . . . until it seemed that

8. For an excellent survey of both Old and New Testament references to the casting of lots in this uniquely Biblical fashion, see the Wikipedia entry for "Urim and Thummim."

its roar would lift the roof off the house and bring the chief priests' henchmen running.

As we wondered ... and waited, for each of us has been conscious daily of our Lord's promise to return to us with the gift of Holy Spirit, the room in which we gathered seemed to become brighter and brighter. I peeked around—I never was much for praying with my eyes closed!—and saw little flickering flames like candlelight hovering over the heads of those around me. It suddenly felt irreverent to try to look up to see whether there was a little flame flickering above my head, too ... but from the strange warming of my own spirit, I sensed that I, too, was somehow alight like the others.

It was an incredible experience. I can't tell you how long it lasted ... or even how it ended. When it was over, I felt—I don't know quite how to say it—whole ... happy ... healthy ... healed, certainly, of the bitterness of disappointment and despair I had been suffering ever since losing the election. I felt inspired (I guess because there was a new spirit within me). I felt encouraged (though my courage was not quite of the sort that seemed to explode some of the others out of the house and into the streets and marketplaces to start witnessing openly to the death and resurrection of the Lord Jesus Christ). I felt empowered—to do what, I wasn't yet sure, but I just knew that I could do almost anything I set my heart and mind and faith to doing!

Miracles are taking place out there. The apostles—of whom I wanted so much to be one—are preaching and teaching and converting and explaining in ways that I cannot imagine, and in languages none of them even know how to speak. Yet I'm strangely content to be here indoors ... alone ... no longer needing the refuge of my garden . . . content to bask in the soft warm afterglow of what I can only think must be, for me, at least, the gift of Holy Spirit.

I don't know that I have ever felt truly "content" before. What a strange and lovely sensation! I am content to feel that my life is in God's hands . . . that my spirit is in Christ's keeping . . . that my eternal destiny is in the everlasting embrace of Holy Spirit. I am quiet—not bored, or resigned, or even complacent. Just the opposite: I am energized . . . optimistic . . . eager to get on with whatever God's providence and Christ's lordship and Holy Spirit's inspiration have in store for me. I am certain now that I was never meant to be an apostle—though I still don't quite know why not—and probably never will.

But I am just as certain that I am meant to be a lifelong follower of the Lord Jesus Christ . . . and that that is . . . and ever will be . . . enough. Spiritual gifts and personal graces sufficient to my calling—whatever it turns out to be—will come to me, I know—if I am patient . . . and faithful . . . and obedient . . . when God provides . . . and Christ claims . . . and Holy Spirit enables . . . whatever ministry or ministries I am meant to have and do and be.

What a wonderful gift: to be able to be still . . . and know that God is God . . . that Jesus is Lord . . . that Holy Spirit is present . . . and that my life has worth . . . and purpose . . . a destiny . . . and a mission that is yet to be revealed.

If you were ever given such a gift, what would you do with—and about—it? If you wanted to receive such a gift, how—and where—would you prepare yourself to receive it?

Why not keep silence with me—here and now—and let

God's Holy Spirit be present . . . and persuasive . . . and power-ful . . . in your heart, and in your faith, and in your life, too?

— XVII —

BARABBAS

BACKGROUND COMMENTARY

T HREE DISTINCT STREAMS of ministry converged in the preparation and first presentation of this Sunday-after-Easter monologue in the Church of St. Andrew and St. Paul in center-city Montreal, Quebec in 1980.

The first, and most immediate, was a Lenten midweek Bible study I had been conducting that year on some of the post-Resurrection "miracles" that had shaped the beginnings of what became the Christian Church. My theme had been "God moves in a mysterious way His wonders to perform."[1] For each study, I had selected a Scripture passage in which a seeming "miracle" might have actually been wrought with the unexpected, and perhaps unnoticed, aid and involvement of one or more human agents. One of the most fascinating of these for my study group was the deliverance of Peter from prison after he had been imprisoned by King Herod Agrippa I in a frenzy of violent suppression of the People of the Way.[2] The group speculated long and hard about the "who" and the "how" of this deliverance—and, at some point in that speculation, I thought of Bar-Abbas, about whom I was even then trying to develop a post-Easter soliloquy.

The second stream of ministry was, in fact, this developing message. In that period in the Province of Quebec, many disaffected Roman Catholics were, for one reason or another, at-

---

1. The first line of William Cowper's famous last hymn, written in 1773 after an almost suicidal bout of depression, and usually set to the tune "Dundee," first published in the *Scottish Psalter* of 1615.
2. Acts 12.

tending the Church of St. Andrew and St. Paul and becoming increasingly active in our work and worship. Out of their French-Canadian Roman Catholic background, they were accustomed to more focus upon the *death* of Jesus than upon his *resurrection*—the *crucifix* rather than the *cross*! I wanted to present a preaching emphasis upon the Calvinist understanding that Jesus Christ died *for me—in my place*—but that that was not the whole story: Jesus Christ also *rose* from the dead for me—for us all!—and his living presence is the motivating factor that energizes the Christian Church and its members to this very day. As I meditated upon the Scriptural testimony that Jesus Bar-Joseph literally died in the place of Jesus Bar-Abbas,[3] I felt that I had found the ideal protagonist to make that preaching point.

The third factor at work in the preparation of this soliloquy—in fact (as I look back over my preserved sermon manuscripts) in the *totality* of my preaching ministry at that time—was the ever-present threat of French-Canadian separatism, and the never-absent sense of personal and political helplessness amongst the English-speaking Canadian minority in the Province of Quebec, of which my congregation was a prominent part. A strong emphasis in my week-to-week preaching was the challenge—and encouragement—to everyone in my ecclesiastical constituency to "make a difference" wherever, whenever, and however they could . . . and to be emboldened to do so in the name and in the faith of our risen and reigning Lord Jesus Christ.

That I succeeded somehow was attested, unexpectedly, two years later. Because of a sermon I had preached against the in-

---

3. See Matthew 27:15-17 as a reference to this intriguing word-play mentioned only in this Gospel passage.

justices of the *Parti Québecois'* Francophone language policies,
I had become an unintentional "spokesman" for the Anglo-
phone minority during the height of the separatism frenzy in
the late 1970s. My life was threatened, as was my wife's and my
children's; my ministerial credibility was undermined; and my
church was on an extremist cadre's "hit list" for bombing if the
referendum on Quebec separatism failed to be approved. At the
beginning of April 1982, I announced that I would be leaving
the Church of St. Andrew and St. Paul, and Montreal, to move
to Toronto to become the General Secretary of the Canadian
Bible Society—a move which created a great deal of disappointment and even animosity amongst those in the congregation
who felt, and not without some justification, betrayed by my
departure from *la belle province* whilst the battle over separatism
was still undecided.

Exhausted by the strain under which I had been living and
working for some time, I proposed to my congregation that I
would present a series of post-Easter "reruns" in the remaining
months of my ministry—repeats of some of the most-requested
sermons from my decade of preaching there—and Bar-Abbas'
soliloquy was the second-most-asked-for message!

I cannot resist also mentioning that, in that sinister summer
of 1980, I had been invited to be a vacationing guest preacher
at the First Presbyterian Church in Chatham, Ontario. (This is
the congregation for which, as I noted in the Preface, the form
and substance of this book finally came together two-and-a-half
decades later.) Frankly, I had all but forgotten that I had presented "Barabbas" on that earlier occasion, along with much of
the explanatory background material I have included above. So

powerful was the soliloquy in the Quebec separatism context in which I had first preached it that some in the Chatham congregation recalled it when I began my "Transformation Testimonies" series 26 summers later!

In the meantime, I had also been privileged to visit the Holy Land on several occasions. During each visit, I was able to descend way below Jerusalem's Convent of the Sisters of *Notre Dame de Sion* to spend time in prayer on the *Lithostrotos*, the exposed paving stones archeologists have determined to be part of the courtyard of the Antonia Fortress—the very place where Pontius Pilate sentenced Jesus to death, and our Lord began his *via dolorosa* to Calvary carrying his own cross. I always find this devotional exercise tremendously moving...and so the Antonia Fortress has come to play an important part in my imagining the characters and circumstances of my monologues.[4]

* * * * *

4. See CHAPTER XI, "What Shall I Do with Him?"

AGENT OF DEATH/ANGEL OF LIFE

The governor again said to them,
"Which of the two do you want me to release for you?"
And they said, "Barabbas."
Pilate said to them,
"Then what should I do with Jesus who is called the Messiah?"
All of them said, "Let him be crucified!
Then he asked, "Why, what evil has he done?"
But they shouted all the more, "Let him be crucified!"

(MATTHEW 27:21-22)

My name is Jesus . . . Jesus Bar-Abbas.[5] Both names are important to me—and important to you if you want to understand what I'm about to do.

I was named "Jesus" after Joshua—the great warrior who
fought the Battle of Jericho and led the children of Israel in the
conquest of the Promised Land.[6] I have always been proud of
that name . . . and, as a young man, I dedicated my life to the re-
conquest of my homeland in the name of the God of Abraham,

5. See Matthew 27, Mark 15:6-15, Luke 23:17-19, and John 18:39-41.
6. See Joshua 6.

Isaac and Jacob.

My other name—Bar-Abbas—I'm not so proud of . . . but it's still an important part of who I am. In Aramaic, *bar-abbas* means literally "son of a father"—and in the back streets of Jerusalem, where I was born and brought up, it is the surname given to children who have no father—at least none anybody knows or knows about. So, *bar-abbas* means "bastard"—and that's what I've been known as all my life.

My mother was a tramp . . . a woman of easy virtue who abandoned me when I was old enough to beg for food in the marketplace and scrounge my night's shelter in the stable of an inn. My biological father was probably a Roman soldier: I have the build of a Roman—not a Jew—and a Roman nose . . . and eyes . . . and hair—features I've put to good use in recent years. But more of that later.

I grew up alone, and tough, and bitter. I've fought for everything I've ever had . . . and I owe no man anything . . . except . . . well, let me tell you the story of how and why I'm doing what I'm doing.

When I was in my teens, I got involved with a gang of revolutionaries who called themselves "Zealots." Their "zeal" was for the freedom of Israel, and their hero was Judas Maccabaeus, who had led a Jewish rebellion that succeeded briefly about a hundred years ago. I found their rhetoric inspiring . . . and their hatred of the Romans infectious . . . and their guerrilla warfare fun . . . and their company the first real friendship I had ever known. I poured all my bitterness . . . all my frustration . . . all my strength . . . all my cunning . . . into the activities of the Zealots.

We robbed Roman merchants and tax collectors . . . and gave the money (well, *some* of the money!) to the poor of Jerusalem. We ganged up on the Roman soldiers we could catch alone or in pairs on the city streets . . . and beat them, and humiliated them, and a couple of times got carried away and actually killed them. We preached hatred, and rebellion, and violence, and plotted ways we could eventually overthrow the Romans and drive them out of Palestine.

I became the leader of the "movement"—I thought that sounded better than "gang"—when Simon, our former leader, abandoned us to follow another street preacher, Jesus of Nazareth, whose "thing" was spiritual—rather than political—revolution, and whose approach promised to change the world by changing the hearts and minds of people, rather than just by changing governments.[7]

I had neither the time nor the patience for that kind of nonsense! Besides, I was working on plans for a really big show of force that I thought might catch the imagination of the uncommitted Jews, and ignite the popular revolution we had been advocating for so long.

Jerusalem's entire water supply was dependent on a network of aqueducts fed by mountain springs outside the city. It had one vulnerable spot: a sluice gate that controlled the whole water flow from a place that was hard to get at—and easy to defend—on a little outcropping of rock on Mount Zion. My plan was to mount a surprise attack on the sluice gate at the time of Passover—when the city would be full of pilgrims—and cut off the water supply until either the Romans abandoned the city or the Jews rose up in rebellion and drove them out.

7. See Matthew 10:4, Mark 3:18, Luke 6:15, and Acts 1:13 where "Simon the Zealot" is listed among Jesus Christ's disciples.

Ironically, it was Jesus of Nazareth and his disciples who provided me an unexpected opportunity to put my plan to the test. They staged a huge demonstration on the first day of the week before Passover and as much as proclaimed Jesus the Messiah in a triumphant procession into Jerusalem.[8] I decided that that was the time to act: the Romans would be distracted by the demonstration . . . and if we failed, which I was sure we would not, the blame for the incident might be shifted onto the Nazarenes.

But I was wrong on all counts. The Roman guard at the sluice gate was stronger than I had expected . . . the demonstration had only made them so alert that our surprise attack failed! To make a long story short, two other Zealots and I were captured, brought before the Roman procurator, or governor, Pontius Pilate, and sentenced to death by crucifixion.

We were imprisoned in the Antonia Fortress garrison near the Temple—and it was my first real exposure to Roman soldiers—other than in brawls, that is. In spite of myself, I was impressed by their discipline and morale, their courage in the face of constant harassment by the Jewish citizenry, and their compassion towards the three of us awaiting execution. The centurion in charge of the garrison took a particular interest in me . . . and we developed a friendship of sorts, even though he was old enough to be my father. It was he, in fact, who first commented on my Roman physique and appearance, and jokingly suggested that maybe I had been fighting on the wrong side!

After four days in prison, suddenly and unaccountably I was released into the custody of the high priest, Caiaphas. At his palace, I was told that Caiaphas had interceded with Pilate to

8. See Matthew 21, Mark 11, and Luke 19.

spare my life—which wasn't exactly true, as I found out later—
and that, to repay the immense debt I owed him, I must become
a "go-between," a secret agent of sorts, between the High Priest
and the Zealots, whose terrorist activities the religious leaders
could not, of course, officially condone but which they very
much wanted to encourage and coordinate nonetheless. I was
to be given a harmless and respectable position in the High
Priest's household and was to lead a circumspect and peaceable
life, while keeping up my Zealot contacts and reporting back
and forth on their conspiracies.

Not many weeks into this new arrangement, I was approached one day by the Roman centurion who had befriended
me in prison. I still felt strangely drawn to him, despite my life-
long hatred of all Romans and my still-burning resentment
against the Roman father who had carelessly fathered me then
never been a father at all. He somehow sensed my ambiguity:
not only about himself and the Romans, but also about the cor-
rupt household in which I was not really enjoying my enforced
respectability. So when he suggested that I become a *double*
agent—or maybe even a *triple* agent—spying for the Romans
on the High Priest for whom I was conspiring with the Zealots,
I was more intrigued than offended . . . and to my surprise, I
agreed.

The centurion and I have met once every other week for all
these years since my release from the Antonia Fortress . . . and
he's become like a father to me. Sometimes I almost wish I could
believe he were my father; then I remember how much I have
always hated the father I never knew . . . and I feel all mixed up
inside.

I feel mixed up about other things, too. The centurion has told me how and why I was really released from prison and saved from execution: how someone also named "Jesus"—Jesus of Nazareth—had been arrested, too, and charged with treason; and how Pilate wanted to set *him* free according to the Passover custom; and how the chief priests and my own Zealots began screaming my name instead, until the crowd took up the cry, and Pilate was forced to give in and set me free instead.[9] So, you see, I actually owe my life not to the High Priest, who has kept me in grateful servitude ever since, but to the Roman governor, who didn't want to release me at all . . . and to this Jesus of Nazareth, who literally died in my place, with my fellow Zealots, one on either side.[10]

The centurion has also told me about Jesus' death, for he commanded the crucifixion squad that afternoon at Calvary. Apparently Jesus died with words of forgiveness and love and despair and faith on his lips. It was so awesome an experience that the centurion believes to this day that he put to death the Son of God.[11]

The followers of Jesus have claimed ever since that their Lord did not stay dead: that he rose from the grave and still lives with them in spirit if not in body. They have turned the world upside down[12] with their teachings about God's love and a new morality based on faith rather than fear . . . and I must confess that I've become more and more interested in what they have to say.

I've become pretty disillusioned with politics as an answer to life's problems. We have a new high priest in Jerusalem, and a new king in Palestine, and a new emperor in Rome—and

9. See Luke 23:13ff.
10. See Luke 23:32ff.
11. See Matthew 27:53-55, Mark 15:38-40, and Luke 23:46-48.
12. See Acts 17:6.

nothing much has changed; if anything, life is harder than ever before. The Zealots are still at it. One of these days they will go too far, though, and bring about the destruction of our city, our culture, and our hopes.

Maybe Jesus of Nazareth was right: the way to change the world is to start with individual people like you and me. The followers of Jesus I have met certainly seem to live in a world of their own: they're kind . . . and gentle . . . and compassionate toward one another . . . and unafraid of what the future may bring—even Herod's persecutions.[13] They believe that their risen Jesus is with them . . . and that God's will gets done despite the worst efforts of people to thwart it.

That's why I've decided to try to rescue a man named Simon Peter, the leader of the followers of Jesus here in Jerusalem. He has been arrested by Herod . . . and put in the Antonia Fortress, where once I was imprisoned. Peter's under constant surveillance . . . and may well be put to death any day now as a calculated desecration of our Passover. I know I can't repay Jesus of Nazareth for dying in my place . . . but maybe I can save Peter's life as my own was once spared.

The squad of soldiers assigned to guard Peter tonight is under the command of my friend, the centurion, and they're all well known to me. They've agreed to help me stage a "miraculous" escape. Herod is so madly suspicious that he will believe a "miracle" far more readily than a plot! If all goes well, by tomorrow morning, Simon Peter should be safely hidden away at the home of his friend, John Mark . . .[14]

. . . and I may be, too. I can't continue the life I've been living. My lies and disloyalties and spying and sneaking around are

---

13. See Acts 12.
14. See Acts 12:11-13.

at an end. I can no longer support the Zealots; I can no longer abide the High Priest and his party; I can no longer find it in my heart to hate the Romans.

Perhaps, if Jesus really does live in the hearts and lives of his followers, he can live in my life, too. If he really did die with words of forgiveness and faith on his lips, perhaps he can forgive me all these years of violence and bitterness and deceit. Perhaps he can even replace all that with real faith in a God who really cares . . . and with genuine hope for a future brightened by confidence . . . and with honest love among people who have too long been at enmity with one another.

It's time for me to slip away to the Fortress. I've never in my life been afraid . . . till now . . . because nothing in my life has ever mattered so much before. I hope—I *know*—that I'm about to try to do a better thing than I have ever done in my life before.

Pray for me . . . and for Simon Peter . . . please!

— XVIII —

CORNELIUS
(PART TWO)

BACKGROUND COMMENTARY

W HEN I WAS MINISTERING to my congregation in suburban Chicago, I had the adventurous privilege of taking a large church group on a pilgrimage to the Holy Lands of the Bible.

The very first place our pilgrimage tour visited in Israel was the site of the outstanding archeological ruins now greatly restored at Caesarea, an old town on the eastern shore of the Mediterranean Sea between Tel Aviv and Haifa—ominously close to where so much recent warfare has been being waged. My favorite spot in Caesarea is a ruined tower tucked away in a windswept corner of the ancient Roman citadel with a breathtaking view of the Mediterranean, and an aura of holiness so real as to be almost inescapable.

This is the traditional site of the home of Cornelius, a centurion (or captain) of the Italian Cohort stationed there in the middle of the first century AD. Because of the narrative recorded in the tenth chapter of the Book of the Acts of the Apostles, the spot is revered by Christians from every nation and tradition and denomination as the place where the Gospel of the Risen Lord Jesus Christ was *first* made known to Gentiles outside the covenant community of Jewry.

The mention in Acts 10:2 that Cornelius was "a devout man who feared God with all his household" has long intrigued me. When I first prepared this message, I created an imaginary identity for Cornelius that brought him into the Imperial Roman army—and the Italian Cohort—as the beneficiary of the patronage of a retired army commander. But as I reworked the soliloquy series for that summer of "Transformation Testimonies" I have already mentioned, I felt inspired to link the identity of this Roman centurion with that other imaginary centurion whom I had placed in Bethlehem at the time of Jesus' birth.[1] From that early experience, it seemed to me, an interest in the Hebrew faith and a devotion to the one God of the Torah tradition would be a very natural life-long outcome. The link is, of course, purely the product of my imagination; the veracity of the story in Acts 10 does not depend on it in any way.

This monologue tries to imagine what it might have felt like to be part of that momentous breakthrough for what soon became our Christian faith and church. The identification of Jesus as "Lord of all" was a critical development in our faith history: difficult for Simon Peter; divisive among the first Jewish believers; ultimately determinative in the sweep of Christianity throughout the then-known world until it became the established religion of the Roman Empire within less than three hundred years.

* * * * *

1. See CHAPTER III, "No Room."

HE IS LORD OF ALL

Then Peter began to speak to them:
"I truly understand that God shows no partiality,
but in every nation
anyone who fears him and does what is right
is acceptable to him.
You know the message he sent to the people of Israel,
preaching peace by Jesus Christ—
he is Lord of all."
(ACTS 10:34-36)

You don't remember me, do you? No . . . I didn't think you would.

It was long ago—thirty years or more—and far away—down in Judea, south of Jerusalem, in a dusty little village named Bethlehem . . . the so-called City of David.

My name is Cornelius . . . and when we met back then, I probably boasted to you that I was the *youngest* centurion ever in the Roman army!

Now I'm surely the *oldest* surviving centurion still on active duty in the Imperial military—way past due for retirement—but kept on here in the fortress of Caesarea at the specific request of the governor, Felix, who has always found me "useful" in his dealings with the Jews, and especially with wily old King Herod Agrippa and his court of priests and lawyers.

You see, ever since that unforgettable experience in Bethlehem thirty-odd years ago, I have felt a special affinity for the Jews . . . and their unusual religion . . . and their unique God. I can still remember telling people—maybe I even told you—how the night that baby was born in the stable of an inn—because I was too self-centered to give up my room—I *knew* somehow—don't ask me *how*, I just *knew*—that I really was in the presence of God.

I found myself kneeling . . . and praying—I, who had never knelt to any save the emperor, and had never prayed to any god I can remember! I prayed to the ancient God of the prophets of Israel, who had promised such a Savior; I prayed to the great God who seemed to have come to me, so powerfully and so personally, in the birth of this helpless baby; I prayed to the mysterious God I felt filling me with a new spirit of peace and joy and faith and hope and love.

And ever since, strange as it may seem for a soldier, I've always been what I guess you can only call "religious." Not *pious* religious . . . nor even *practicing* religious . . . more like *superstitious* religious . . . and maybe a little *curious* religious. I've always offered the usual sacrifices to the whole panoply of pagan Roman gods: hey, what's a bit of meat, or a cup of wine, or a few coins here or there? If it might do me some good with the gods, why not? And, as a soldier, I have to pledge allegiance to the emperor as a god—though we all know that's gotten to be more of a bad joke than a gesture of good faith!

And I think it's ironic that, throughout my military career with the Italian Cohort, the roughest, toughest regiment in the Roman Army, I've actually been more of a diplomat than a soldier. Between occasional tours of duty back in Rome, I've actually spent much of my life here in Syria, at one posting or another, always with some connection to or responsibility for the Jewish community wherever it was. A few years ago, after the death of King Herod Agrippa, when it looked as though the Jews might organize a real rebellion, our cohort was posted more or less permanently to the fortress here at Caesarea.[2]

This citadel is like a city within a city—so strong and so spacious that I've finally been able to have my wife and children come from Italy to join me. We have a suite of rooms in one of the towers overlooking the Mediterranean Sea... and, for a soldier, this is about as good a posting as you can get.

Since we've been in Caesarea, my wife has become friends with some of the Jewish women whose husbands do business in the citadel... and she's learned a lot about their religion... and their practices... and their almsgiving to relieve the poor and needy. I've been able to go to their synagogue services more than a few times... and I've studied their Torah laws... and I've supported many of their charities. But I've never presented myself as a proselyte for conversion: that would require ritual *circumcision*—and, although I'm fearless about facing a man armed with a sword, I'm not about to submit to a rabbi armed with a scalpel!

What really attracts me to the faith of the Jews, because

---

2. A historical fact recorded in *The Interpreter's Bible*, VOL. IX, p. 133.

somehow it harks back to that life-defining night in Bethlehem, is their insistence upon there being only *one* God—not a whole host of legendary deities—but a *creator* God who loves His creation and has entered into a mutual covenant with His "Chosen People" to bless and prosper them in proportion to their worship of and faithfulness to Him alone. Given the hard times the Jews have gone through during so much of their history, I guess they must not be doing too well in the way of *obedience*: but they keep looking forward to the coming of the One they call the *Messiah*—"the promised One"—who will restore them to God's good graces again.

So you can imagine how intrigued I was a few months ago to hear reports that, up in Damascus, and down in Joppa, the synagogues were full of talk that the Messiah had come! I felt myself being drawn to the hope that this might be true . . . and that in my lifetime I might see God's Chosen People blessed by a king who could give them enough political stability and economic prosperity that there wouldn't be a need for the Italian Cohort to be stationed in Caesarea anymore, and I might retire on my accumulated booty and live out my life with my wife and family in this little bit of seaside heaven on earth.

I began to pray about it—really *pray*—not just recite empty words and memorized phrases—trying to tell this *one God* how much *I* would like for His *Messiah* to come and redeem His people . . . and in the process set me really free, too. And, of course, without ever saying a word about it to anyone—even my wife!—I wondered, and hoped, and even prayed that this One, this Messiah, would turn out to be a thirty-something savior who happened to have been born in Bethlehem during the time of the census when Quirinius was governor of Syria![3]

One day last week, about three o'clock in the afternoon before I went on duty, I was praying that way in my room when I had what I can only describe as a "vision." I clearly saw what had to have been "an angel of God" coming in and calling me by name. I confess: I stared at him in terror and blurted out, "What is it?"

He answered, "Your prayers and your alms have ascended as a memorial before God. Now send men to Joppa for a certain Simon who is called Peter . . ."[4]

I did as the apparition commanded. I sent two of my slaves and a soldier I knew to be as interested in things "religious" as I was to Joppa to bring this Simon Peter back with them. Later, I learned that Simon Peter was very loath to come. He is a strict Jew, and though he has a wonderful story to tell, he had always assumed that it was to be told to the Jews only . . . and not to uncircumcised Gentiles like me.

But apparently he had had a vision, too—a far more complicated and troubling one than mine—that convinced him that it was all right (in fact, it was God's will) that he should come to Caesarea and to my home and family and share his good news with us Gentiles for the very first time.[5] So he came, bringing with him a few of the believers from Joppa, not without doubts and fears but also with a clear conviction that his God "shows no partiality, but that in every nation anyone who fears God and does what is right is acceptable to him."[6]

I gathered my family together and a few friends who I thought might be interested in what Simon Peter had to say and told him "So now we're all here in God's presence, ready to listen

3. Luke 2:1-2.
4. Acts 10:4-6.
5. Acts 10:9-23.
6. Acts 10:34-35.

to whatever the Lord has put in your heart to tell us."[7]
I'll never forget how he started right in:

> *You know the message he sent to the people of Israel,*
> *preaching peace by Jesus Christ—he is Lord of all.*
> *That message spread throughout Judea, beginning in*
> *Galilee after the baptism that John announced: how*
> *God anointed Jesus of Nazareth with the Holy Spirit*
> *and with power; how he went about doing good and*
> *healing all who were oppressed by the devil, for God*
> *was with him.*
>
> > *We are witnesses to all that he did both in Judea*
> *and in Jerusalem. They put him to death by hanging*
> *him on a tree; but God raised him on the third day*
> *and allowed him to appear, not to all the people but*
> *to us who were chosen by God as witnesses, and who*
> *ate and drank with him after he rose from the dead.*
> *He commanded us to preach to the people and to tes-*
> *tify that he is the one ordained by God as judge of the*
> *living and the dead. All the prophets testify about him*
> *that everyone who believes in him receives forgiveness*
> *of sins through his name.*[8]

But, most of all, I'll never forget how I felt when Simon
Peter said, "Jesus Christ: He is Lord of all"—not just for the
Jews . . . but for everyone! It was as though the one God to
whom I had been praying all this time was speaking right to my
heart and soul and mind, and saying "Jesus Christ: He is Lord
of all" . . . of *you*, Cornelius, and your wife, and your children,
and your friends, and your colleagues, and your whole world!
He is not a king, as the world recognizes kings . . . and His reign

---

7. Acts 10:33.
8. Acts 10:34-43.

is not going to be one of political and economic prosperity. He is your Lord . . . your Redeemer . . . your Savior . . . your Friend.

I didn't understand then—I still don't understand altogether—the significance of Jesus Christ's rising from the dead . . . except that I know, somehow, that my Redeemer lives . . .⁹ that my Savior reigns victorious over life and death . . . and that my life has taken on a meaning and a measure that extend far beyond what I thought was this little corner of heaven on earth . . . right into all eternity. My wife feels it too: we both have experienced such a sense of forgiveness . . . such a sense of peace . . . such a sense of confidence . . . since Simon Peter told us that Jesus Christ is *our* Lord, and that His sacrifice on the cross was *for us*, as much as for anyone else, and that His resurrection opens *to us* a whole new universe of faith and hope and love beyond anything we ever thought "religion" could be about!

The others in the room felt it, as well. One of them said that it was as though a spirit of holiness had come over us. Simon Peter laughed, and said that that was exactly what he and the Lord's other disciples had called it when it had first happened to them: a spirit of holiness, a "Holy Spirit" that seems to be the gift of the risen Christ to all who believe in Him and accept His lordship over their lives.

Someone with Peter suggested that we ought to be "baptized." We didn't know what that meant, but when they explained that it was an outward sign with water to signify an inward cleansing of our souls and a dying to our old selves so that we could be born again as new followers of this new Lord, we agreed and were baptized that very day "in the name of Jesus

9. Job 19:25.

Christ."[10]

Now Simon Peter has set off for Jerusalem, to tell the other leaders of "the Way" about us Gentiles and our acceptance of Jesus Christ as Lord and Savior. In his absence, I realize that everything is just the way it was before he came . . . and yet nothing seems the same. I still have a job to do, and a century of the cohort to command, and the prospect of retirement is probably still as distant as ever.

But that Holy Spirit still glows within my heart, too . . . and my mind is still full of the knowledge of the glory of God revealed in the teachings of Jesus . . . and my eyes look at my world and at my wife and family and friends and colleagues—and even at myself—from a whole new perspective, with a whole new set of values and a whole new list of priorities and a whole new expectation of what tomorrow may bring . . . and the tomorrow after that . . . until all our tomorrows merge into eternity.

"Jesus Christ: He is Lord of all!" That simple sentence . . . that good news in a nutshell . . . changed my life . . . and it's already beginning to change my world.

What about you? . . . and your life? . . . and your world? Jesus Christ—risen, reigning, loving, leading—is he *your* Lord too? Does that make any difference to you? . . . to those around you? . . . to the world in which you live? I hope it *does*!

Think about it. That's an order!

---

10. Acts 10:44-48.

— XIX —

JULIUS

BACKGROUND COMMENTARY

T HE SECOND EPISTLE OF Saint Paul to the Corinthians
contains a Bible verse that took on particular significance for me over the couple of years in which my late
wife and I battled problems I never knew—never even suspected—I would have to face: problems physical, mental, emotional, spiritual, vocational.

"When I am weak, then I am strong," is a motto so self-con-
tradictory as to sound, at first, more like foolishness than like
faith. But it comes at the end of a long and complicated passage
in Paul's second letter to the Christians in Corinth in which the
Apostle finds himself forced to defend himself against enemies
of the faith who have attacked his apostolic credentials and even
his spiritual authority to preach the Gospel of the Lord Jesus
Christ. Paul admits that it is folly to boast; but boast he does:
about the five times he has been whipped thirty-nine lashes at
the hands of the Jews . . . about the three times he has been
beaten with rods . . . about the time he was stoned . . . about the
shipwrecks . . . and the dangers of travel . . . and the occasions
of hunger, thirst, cold and exposure that have distinguished his
career as a missionary for the Gospel.[1]

Finally, Paul confesses to a weakness (whether physical, or
emotional, or mental, or spiritual he never really says), calling
it "a thorn . . . in the flesh, a messenger of Satan," given to harass

---

1. 2 Corinthians 11:23-27.

and humiliate him before God and man.[2] Thrice he has prayed to be released from this infirmity, he admits; and thrice God has denied his prayer, saying, "My grace is sufficient for you, and my power is made perfect in weakness."[3]

Because these words came to mean so much to me, and because we all live in a topsy-turvy world in which they might mean so much to so many others, I wanted to try to "put this across" in a way that could be intriguing to young people and older adults alike. So I imagined a first-person version of the Biblical story told in the 27th and 28th chapters of the Book of the Acts of the Apostles, adopting the point of view of the fictional centurion who would have commanded the unit of troops ordered to accompany Paul and his party from Syria to Rome.

As a sailor, I delighted in researching this chronicle of Paul's third missionary journey, and hoped that the nautical details I included would make the story "come alive" for some of the men in the congregation who loved sailing as much as I did.

As tempting as it was to try to identify this Roman centurion with one of the other men of that profession who have come to life in my other monologues,[4] I found as I worked the texts for this sermon that "Julius" was "his own man"—with a unique point of view that resisted any effort on my part to link him with any of the Gospel incidents in which Roman centurions played a part.

For as the message took shape, I eventually realized that in Julius I had the useful perspective of a *non-believer*—one who could ask some of the hard and unanswerable questions about *how* and *why* God can do, or at least allow, "bad things to hap-

---

2. 2 Corinthians 12:7.
3. 2 Corinthians 12:8-9.
4. See CHAPTERS III, XVII, XVIII, and XX. Clearly, the occasional Gospel appearance of various Roman centurions has been a useful motif for my collection of soliloquies and monologues.

pen to good people," questions we all are tempted to ask at times of terrible stress in our lives or in our world. In that same vein, I was able to have Julius ask the ironic questions at the end of the monologue that questioned whether Paul's determination to reach Rome had been an exercise in futility . . . or had been, as Julius could not yet know, the proclamation of the Gospel at a time and in a place that resulted in Christianity becoming the established religion of the Roman Empire within three centuries.

* * * * *

Weakness and Strength

My grace is sufficient for you,
for my power is made perfect in weakness.
(2 CORINTHIANS 12:9A)

Welcome to Malta ... and to the home of my father-in-law, Publius, the *protos* or "chief man" of the Roman government here on the island.

My name is Julius. I settled on Malta about two years ago ... after having been shipwrecked here a few months earlier. I was badly injured in that wreck ... and was brought to this very house to recuperate ... and Publius' daughter, Claudia, was my nurse ... and, well, you know how those things turn out sometimes.

I've just had a letter from Rome that has brought back many memories of how I first came to Malta ... and of the remarkable man with whom I shared that shipwreck adventure. His name was Paul—and he has apparently just been sentenced to death by the emperor, Nero, on the grounds that he refused to worship the goddess Roma and the divine Caesars our government tells us are all gods.

That really surprises me—not that Paul refused to worship Roma and the Caesars (that's no surprise at all!)—but that he ended up being sentenced to death! Paul's greatest ambition in life was to testify before the emperor; his deepest conviction was that, if he could only have a chance to tell his story to the imperial court, he would win the whole world to his new religion.

Paul's determination to get to Rome was the reason for our being thrown together in the first place. He was a prisoner of Porcius Festus at Caesarea; and when his trial seemed to be getting nowhere, and Festus would neither acquit him nor sentence him, Paul suddenly appealed—by his right as a Roman citizen—to appear before the emperor to state his case.[5] At that time, I was a young centurion in the Augustan cohort—a sort of auxiliary or militia unit stationed in Syria. I was ambitious . . . and anxious to see the world . . . so, when I heard that there was an important prisoner to be escorted to Rome, I volunteered for the assignment.

It didn't turn out to be nearly as glamorous a trip as I had anticipated! I was given custody of a whole contingent of prisoners bound for Rome of whom Paul was only one. He had the privileges of *custodia libera*—a sort of "house arrest"—and was accompanied by an *amanuensis*, or secretary, and a Macedonian manservant. They were to have the best cabins on our ships and the freedom to visit and receive friends *en route*, all on the direct orders of Porcius Festus, who seemed to be of the opinion that Paul had been wrongfully accused and arrested and could have been set free altogether had he not been so determined to ap-

5. See Acts 25.

pear before Nero to state his case.

Our voyage from Caesarea started out pleasantly enough. Although it was fairly late in the shipping season, I managed to secure adequate passage for my soldiers and prisoners and all aboard a Mysian ship sailing home to Adramyttium. At that time of year, the prevailing winds in the eastern Mediterranean are from the west—which is the direction we had to go to reach Rome—so we traveled northward, and rounded the topmost corner of Cyprus, and took advantage of the offshore breezes to tack our way to Myra in Lycia.

Knowing that we would have to change ships eventually, I was glad to find an Alexandrian grain freighter harbored at Myra just preparing to set sail for Rome. It was the biggest ship I had ever seen—with accommodations for almost three hundred passengers and crew—so I quickly booked passage for my entire entourage and hurried them aboard.

Despite the lateness of the season, the owner and the captain of the freighter both seemed confident that we could make Rome before winter set in. But they were soon proved wrong: we had great difficulty navigating even past Rhodes and Cnidus . . . and when we hit the open waters of the Aegean, a strong northwest wind came sweeping down and threatened to blow us onto the northern coast of Crete. The captain decided to go with the wind instead and sail around to the south of Crete, there to take advantage of the sheltered lee and try to sail westward.

Eventually, we made it to a port named "Fair Havens"—a terrible misnomer for a barren rocky cove with only a few stunted trees and thorny bushes, but a secure and sheltered harbor nonetheless. Because the safe navigation season was well past, many of the sailors began murmuring that they wanted to stay the winter at Fair Havens. I was appalled at the suggestion . . . and the captain wanted to press on at least as far as Phoenix, a better harbor farther west along the southern coast of Crete. At this point, Paul, who had kept pretty much to himself throughout the journey, made me very angry by telling the captain and crew about a vision he had had, in which, he said, his God had told him that there would be much injury and even more loss, if the journey were continued at that time.

Needless to say, the captain and I prevailed, and we set sail for Phoenix on a deceptively gentle offshore breeze. But as soon as we were at sea, a terrible northeaster came down upon us and drove us southwest around the island of Cauda. In the lee of that godforsaken place, the sailors managed to secure the life boat and undergird the ship with great ropes to prevent it from breaking in two when its heavy cargo was lifted out of the water by the tumultuous waves.

Afraid that we might be driven even farther southward and onto the great sandbank off the North African coast, the captain had the sea anchors lowered and all the canvas, save for the small foresail, reefed up. On and on we lurched, driven by the storm. The captain ordered all the loose cargo overboard . . . and then all the ship's extra spars and tackle. There was no respite from the storm . . . and soon we abandoned any hope of ever being saved.

All except Paul. When the storm was at its very worst, he appeared on deck and began to speak to the officers and men. He reminded them of the vision that had warned them to stay at Fair Havens—not in an "I told you so" sort of way—but more as an authentication of the rest of what he had to say. He had had another vision: it was, apparently, God's will that he should safely stand one day before the emperor in Rome; for that reason, everyone sailing with him would be saved . . . though the ship would have to be run aground on some island and be lost.

Paul encouraged us all to eat something; he himself set an example by breaking a slab of hardtack as though it were a fresh-baked loaf . . . said a prayer of thanksgiving to his God . . . and ate a few bites before sharing it with those nearby. As he did so, the sea-swells seemed to ease off a little, and everyone found enough appetite to swallow a mouthful or two. Thus strengthened—in spirit as well as in body, I'd say—the sailors set to throwing some of the wheat into the sea . . . to lighten the ship . . . as though they really had hope again.

Paul went back to his cabin . . . and I followed . . . fascinated by the courage and faith and inspiring leadership he had shown. Before, I had just dismissed him as a Jewish religious fanatic . . . an aristocrat with nothing better to do than cause trouble for us Romans . . . a coward who had tried to prevent us from leaving Fair Havens because he was beginning to get nervous about his long-awaited appearance before Nero.

All through that day . . . and late into the night . . . we talked—mostly about Paul, and his new religion, and his Lord, Jesus, whom he said was the Son of God and the savior of the world. Paul told me how this Jesus had preached faith and hope and love as the three greatest qualities of human life . . . and how he had been put to death by the Roman governor of Judea, Pontius Pilate, on trumped-up charges much like those the Jews had made against himself.

Paul shared with me the story of his conversion, and of his preaching and teaching and missionary journeys throughout Asia Minor and Greece. He recounted the beatings he had suffered at the hands of those who opposed his "good news" about Jesus' resurrection from the dead and living lordship over all of life . . . the imprisonments . . . the dangerous voyages . . . the shipwrecks . . . the exhaustion and hunger and cold and exposure . . . the hostility and rejection of so many of his fellow Jews . . . the suspicion and animosity of so many of the civil and religious authorities in the Gentile communities he had visited . . . even the physical ailment—the "thorn in the flesh," he called it—which pained and troubled him constantly.

And then he told me something I have never forgotten. He claimed that it was always in those very times of danger and difficulty that he felt God nearest, and saw clearest that his weakness could become the occasion for God's strength to be revealed. "When I am weak, then I am strong," he said again and again; "for when I confess that I no longer have the wherewithal to succeed on my own, I discover that God has the will . . . and the way . . . to make His plans and purposes succeed." That was why he was so confident that he . . . and I . . . and my soldiers and prisoners . . . and the captain and crew . . . would all reach shore safely . . . despite our apparent danger: because Paul knew that he had a date with destiny in Rome—and God would bring the impossible to pass.

And Paul was right. As the next day dawned, he went on deck again to encourage the men to eat a little more. In the gathering light, we spied a bay with a beach on some as-yet-unrecognized island . . . which turned out to be Malta. The captain changed course and ran full with the wind and the waves toward the beckoning shoreline. At the mouth of the bay, we struck an unseen shoal: the bow stuck fast on the bottom . . . the waves pounded the stern . . . the ship began to break up.

Hearing the captain's order to abandon ship, my soldiers wanted to kill all our prisoners, lest any of them escape in the confusion . . . and we find ourselves in double jeopardy for having failed in our duty. But I couldn't let Paul die—not when his life's goal seemed once again within reach—and I couldn't make an exception against a general execution order. So I commanded that all of the prisoners be spared . . . and that each man on his own try to swim to shore on a piece of plank or a broken spar.

It was every man for himself! As I stood by the rail, encouraging Paul and his two companions to jump into the raging sea, a section of the rigging collapsed . . . and a falling timber struck me on the head and shoulder. I went down in a blaze of pain and frustration and blissful unconsciousness. I awakened on the beach beside a roaring bonfire . . . to learn that every single person on the ship had been saved . . . and that I owed my own life to the quick thinking and courageous efforts of my prisoner, Paul, and his Macedonian manservant.

My head ached . . . and my shoulder was broken . . . and I was soon installed here at Publius' house to be nursed back to health by my beloved Claudia. Paul's amanuensis turned out to be a physician, who set my shoulder expertly and almost miraculously healed Publius' father . . . so that his fame spread throughout the islands, and he spent a busy—but profitable—winter curing the local aches and pains. In early spring, my sol-

diers and their prisoners set off for Rome—without me, I'm ashamed to say—and completed their assignment.

I should have kept in touch; after all, Paul did save my life. But I was so sure that the emperor would acquit him . . . and I would have a happy excuse to write. Or he might even visit Malta on his way back to Syria . . . and now he's dead . . . and I'm too late.

"When I am weak, then I am strong." I guess it didn't turn out that way for Paul. What did he accomplish by going to Rome and appearing before the emperor? Obviously, no one listened; no one believed; no one will ever hear of Paul's "good news"—or Paul's "Jesus Christ"—again!

His faith was so strong! His hope was so convincing! His love was so real! How can God—if there is a God—let such a life . . . such a witness . . . such a power . . . just die? . . . and disappear from the face of the earth?

"When I am weak, then I am strong." Who's ever going to listen to "good news" like that again? Who's going to believe in a Lord whose promise is nothing more than that? Would *you*? *Would* you?

— XX —

LOUKAS

BACKGROUND COMMENTARY

L ECTIONARY PREACHING HAS proven to be one of the
most enduring—and intriguing—of the undercurrents
that powered the tidal wave of liturgical change over-
sweeping Protestant Christianity in the second half of the last
century. That preachers would willingly submit themselves to
the rigors of preaching *only* from a repetitive three-year cycle of
arbitrarily assigned Scripture passages was virtually unthinkable
in the mainstream denominations of North America at the mid-
point of the twentieth century and would have been nearly
anathema in the evangelical, Pentecostal, and non-denominational churches that were only just beginning to grow in size
and influence had anyone been so foolhardy as even to have suggested such a thing!

In my recollection, at least three different and very diverse
ecclesiastical streams fed that tidal wave. The first was the phe-
nomenal success of the Revised Standard Version of the Bible.
Published in 1952 by the National Council of Churches of
Christ in the United States of America, the RSV was the first
contemporary language translation of the whole Bible to seriously challenge the authority of the Authorized (or King James)
Version that had held worldwide sway in English-speaking
Protestant Christianity for almost 350 years. Suddenly, the notion of speaking *of*—let alone *to*—*God* in other than Eliza-

bethan verbiage was at least debatable. That debate soon generated an outpouring of prayers, liturgies, and hymns couched in everyday English words and phrases, and "liturgical renewal" took on a whole new meaning.

A spate of other modern-language English Bible translations followed—chief among them the *Good News Bible* (Today's English Version) published by the United Bible Societies, and the New International Version offered by the International Bible Society—bringing with them, almost inevitably, additional and on-going debates about gender inclusive language and politically correct sensibility, none of which have, as yet, totally abated.

The second stream of influence in the storm surge of liturgical renewal was the Consultation on Church Union (COCU). Begun in 1962 as an effort to form an organic union of almost a dozen North American Protestant denominations, COCU managed to impress upon us all the similarities, as much as the differences, amongst the participating churches. Reformed churchfolk began to explore the significance of Anglican and Lutheran episcopacies and liturgies, while their hierarchically ordained and oriented clergy colleagues explored the ramifications of essentially democratic forms of church government. The movement toward organic unity eventually faltered after two decades, and dissolved itself into an ecumenical entity calling itself Churches Uniting in Christ (CUIC).

But the lasting legacy of COCU was the effort that came to be known as the Consultation on Common Texts, the third stream influencing the rise of interest in lectionary preaching. Among the many changes wrought in and to the Roman

Catholic Church by the Second Vatican Council, few have im-
pacted Protestant Christianity more than the introduction in
1969 of a modern-day plan of Bible readings spread over three
years and read in the vernacular of each country, rather than in
Latin. This innovation led directly to the development and publication of the Common Lectionary, published in 1983, which
offered Anglican, Lutheran, and Reformed preachers as well as
Roman Catholic homilists, common ground on which to base
their Sunday sermons. (American Episcopalians stood by the
lectionary in their own Book of Common Prayer until much
more recently!)

The lectionary's repeating three-year cycles of readings—
especially the Synoptic Gospel readings from Matthew in Year
A, Mark (with little supplements from John) in Year B, and
Luke in Year C (with the Gospel of John interspersed in the
liturgical seasons of Advent, Christmas, Epiphany, Lent, Easter
and Pentecost) encouraged preachers to explore the common-
alities as well as the distinctiveness of the four Gospels. And that
is where, when, how and why this soliloquy sermon came into
being.

Early in my ministry at the Church of St. Andrew and St.
Paul in Montreal, we dedicated and placed in the pew-racks the
newly-published Canadian Presbyterian *Book of Praise*. Suddenly, the old bedraggled King James pew Bibles looked, well,
old and bedraggled. Wanting to introduce my new congregation
to the still-in-progress *Good News for Modern Man* New Testament translation of the American Bible Society, and curious
about the viability of "lectionary" preaching in my new situation, I undertook to preach from the Gospel of Luke for the

whole of church year "C."

I bought hundreds of inexpensive "portions" of Luke, published by the Canadian Bible Society on newsprint paper with those delightful little Annie Vallotton line drawings illustrating so many passages, and placed them throughout the sanctuary. I encouraged people to "do the unthinkable": to make notes and highlights and doodles right on the pages of these little scripture portions—even to allow their children to *colour* [*sic*: this was in *Canada*, remember!] the line drawings!

And I introduced the sermon series with this soliloquy. I wanted my people to identify the writer of the Gospel of Luke and the Book of the Acts of the Apostles as an educated Greek-speaking Gentile, a medical student if not a doctor, an eye-witness to Gospel events, both in the Galilee and in Jerusalem, of which the other evangelists may not have been aware, and a worthy traveling companion and amanuensis for the Apostle Paul.

MY INTRODUCTION TO THE SCRIPTURE READINGS
FOR THIS MESSAGE

For today's Scripture lessons, I want you to begin to travel back in imagination to first-century Palestine . . . to the time when Jesus lived on earth and conducted his ministry among the common people of Galilee and Judea. I would like to invite you to meet the young man who, in my imagination, grew up to become the writer of the Bible books we know as the Gospel according to Luke and the Acts of the Apostles.

Perhaps you've never thought about where the Bible's contents came from . . . or what it might have felt like to be one of the people whose writings came to be considered sacred. Perhaps you've just assumed that the Holy Spirit took over, put the writer's hand on autopilot . . . and the Word of God came out the end of the pen.

Our Reformed theology takes the Word of God much more seriously than that. We acknowledge the *inspiration* of the Holy Spirit upon the Holy Bible, but we also acknowledge the *humanity* and *historicity* of the women and men whose literary creations the books of the Bible originally were. So, here is your chance—again, let me stress, out of the fertility of my own imagination—to meet one such person who might have been a creator of Holy Scripture.

During my monologue, I hope you will listen for allusions and references to other stories from other Gospel sources: there are at least a dozen of them. And I hope you will enjoy getting to know the young man whose story, I think, might have begun not in the Gospel of Luke, as you might have expected, but in the *first* written account of the life and ministry of Jesus—the Gospel according to Mark—from which I'm going to read three brief passages: first, Mark 6:30-44; then Mark 14:43-52; and finally, Mark 15:33-39.

* * * * *

AN ORDERLY ACCOUNT

Since many have undertaken to set down an orderly account
of the events that have been fulfilled among us,
just as they were handed on to us by those who from the beginning
were eyewitnesses and servants of the word
I too decided, after investigating everything carefully
from the very first, to write an orderly account for you,
most excellent Theophilus,
so that you may know the truth concerning the things
about which you have been instructed.
(LUKE 1:1-4)

Hello . . . I'm Loukas!

Actually, my real name is Lucanus. My parents are Roman, so I have a Latin name: but since I've come to study here at the University of Athens, I've started using the Greek version. You know—when in Athens, do as the Athenians do!

You've caught me reading a letter from my father. He's a professional soldier—a centurion of the Imperial Roman

Army—just finishing up a five-year posting in Palestine. And none too soon, I guess, from the way he writes: the constant squabbling between the Romans and the Jews has really been getting on his nerves.

The last straw, apparently, was an execution he had to carry out last month on the orders of Pontius Pilate, the proconsul. The Jews persuaded Pilate to put to death a young Galilean rabbi, Jesus of Nazareth, and my father was in charge of carrying out the crucifixion. It must have really got to my dad: he came away convinced that the rabbi was innocent of the charges of blasphemy and sedition . . . and probably was what the country folk claimed he was—the Son of God.[1]

What made it particularly hard for my father was that this wasn't the first time the rabbi, Jesus, had come into our family's life. He wrote most of this letter to explain why he had me hustled out of Jerusalem and on my way to Athens right before "all hell broke loose" for him last month . . . and to remind me of those early encounters with Jesus . . . as though I could ever forget!

We lived in Capernaum when I was a boy, in a really nice house not far from the Roman army barracks. We didn't pay much attention when Jesus and his disciples first came to town; we were Romans after all, and the religion of the Jews was of no interest to us! But I couldn't help overhearing the servants' chatter about this remarkable young man from Nazareth. They said he was a wise and interesting teacher—better than the rabbis in the synagogues or even the professors in the universities. They told how he could work miracles, like healing fevers[2] . . . and leprosy[3] . . . and paralysis[4] . . . and how he had once shown some

---

1. Luke 23:47-8.
2. Luke 4:39.
3. Luke 5:13.
4. Luke 5:18ff.

fishermen how to catch a whole boatload of fish after they had worked all night and caught nothing![5]

Around that time, our houseman, Erastus, fell ill . . . seriously ill. I know now that it was pneumonia. It came on so suddenly and laid Erastus so low, that we were all sure that he was going to die. The army doctors did everything they could think of—Erastus was my father's favorite slave, and they wanted to please the centurion even more than they wanted to heal the servant—but nothing seemed to make any difference.

Finally, I went to my father and suggested that he ask the help of this Jesus of Nazareth about whom I had been hearing so much. After all, I reasoned with adolescent naïveté, if Jesus could heal Jews, why not Gentiles, too? At first, my father hesitated. Then, in desperation, he sent for the leaders of the local synagogue—which he had paid to have built, by the way—and asked their advice about going to Jesus for help. The elders approved the idea, and offered to approach Jesus on my father's behalf.

Later that day, one of the servants rushed in to report that Jesus was on his way to our house to see Erastus! My father was horrified: he's a very humble man within himself, even though he's a tough commanding officer . . . and he couldn't imagine receiving a famous Jewish rabbi with the proper protocol on such short notice. He sent aides to intercept Jesus with the suggestion that the rabbi simply command that Erastus be healed—even at a distance—and that would suffice. And, believe it or not, that's exactly what happened: I don't know what Jesus said or did . . . he certainly didn't ever come to the house . . . but from that day and hour, Erastus began to get better.[6]

5 Luke 5:2ff.
6. Luke 7:1-10.

I was fascinated . . . and determined to see this Jesus up close for myself. That determination was only heightened as, day after day, Capernaum was abuzz with stories of other wondrous things Jesus had done. He faced down the most self-righteous Pharisee in the Galilee at a dinner party in Simon's own home and allowed the most notorious woman in town to kiss his feet before he forgave her of her sins and sent her on her way in peace.[7] He calmed the Sea of Galilee when one of its fast-gathering storms threatened to swamp the little fishing boat in which he and some of his friends were trying to cross over to the territory of Gerasa.[8]

But my fascination reached fever pitch when I heard how Jesus had restored the sanity of a man the people over there thought was demon-possessed. The Gerasenes told and re-told the story so often that it soon became embellished with fanciful details like a legion of demons stampeding a herd of pigs.[9] But somehow, I knew better . . . and I knew that I had to see and hear and maybe even meet this wonderworker whose medical skills outshone anything the best doctors in the Galilee could accomplish!

A few days later, I learned that Jesus and his disciples were at Bethsaida, a village a few miles away along the north shore of the Sea of Galilee.[10] I asked our cook to pack me a hearty lunch, told my parents that I was going for a hike, and set off for Bethsaida.

The crowd that gathered to hear Jesus teach and preach was unbelievable: there must have been at least 5,000 people spread out over the hillside in the hot sun. Jesus spoke about his rela-

7. Luke 7:36-50.
8. Luke 8:22-25.
9. Luke 8:26-39. I added this reference to the Gerasene demoniac only recently to acknowledge the lectionary preaching of a neighbor pastor whose pulpit I was filling on the Sunday this passage was referenced in the Revised Common Lectionary.
10. Luke 9:10ff.

tionship with God—whom he called his father—and about God's love for His children—whom I took to be us—and about a life that would never end, even after death, for those who believed Jesus' teachings and trusted their lives to his love and leadership.

It was so exciting and so beautiful and so convincing that no one thought of anything else all day. Even when it began to get dark, and the cool of the evening made people remember how hungry they were, no one wanted to leave. I unpacked my lunch . . . which I hadn't touched at all (except for some figs I nibbled at noontime) . . . but the hungry stares of those around me made me realize guiltily that most of the people there had nothing to eat.

Jesus' disciples began wandering through the crowd trying to find enough food to put together at least a snack for everyone. Philip, one of the disciples from Capernaum—and a man I had never thought was very bright—looked at my picnic, laughed, and said, "That's hardly enough for a growing boy. You'd best keep it for yourself!"

Then Andrew, Simon Peter's brother,[11] came over and asked me whether I would be willing to contribute my barley buns and dried fish to whatever else they could collect for the common meal. I gave them to him gladly; but you can imagine my surprise—and embarrassment—when they turned out to be the only food the disciples found.

Andrew laughed apologetically as he gave them to Jesus, but the rabbi took them and told the people to sit down for supper and said a blessing over my bread and fish as though they were a banquet and began to break the buns into pieces and pass

11. John 6:1-14.

them among us. Each took a piece—first the bread, and then
the fish—broke it in half, kept one portion, and passed the other
on. In a crescendo of murmuring wonderment, we were all
served ... and ate our fill ... and watched in amazement as the
disciples gathered up the leftovers ... twelve basketsful![12]

To this day, I don't know how Jesus did it. My father has always said there must have been a trick: you may be able to heal
people with miracles, but you can't feed them! I'm not so sure!
I followed Jesus around Galilee for a year or so, watching him
do a lot of wonderful things to people's bodies and minds and
souls, and I don't see why a miracle of feeding should be so
much harder than a miracle of healing. He once said that he
would rise from the dead. I'm willing to believe he could do
even that ... and maybe he has, by this time, for all I know!

Seeing all those miracles and sensing how much Jesus cared
about people has had a tremendous impact on my life. I decided
I wanted to become a doctor, so I can heal people, too ... if not
by miracles, then at least by medicine. Then, even though it
would cost my parents a small fortune, last month they suddenly insisted on my coming to Athens to the best medical
school in the world, right after that embarrassing incident in
the Garden of Gethsemane.

I knew that Jesus and his disciples were in Jerusalem for the
Jewish festival of Unleavened Bread.[13] There had been a tremendous uproar the day they arrived,[14] and my father's century was
on full alert against any possibility of an uprising. I also knew
that Jesus was staying over on the far side of the Mount of Olives
at a home in Bethany, and that it was his custom[15] to cut
through the Garden of Gethsemane on his way back from the

12. Luke 9:10-17.
13. Luke 22:1ff.
14. Luke 19:28ff.
15. Luke 22:39ff.

Temple every night. I wanted so much to talk to him . . . to tell him about my hopes of becoming a doctor and how he had long been my inspiration . . . but my father insisted that it was too dangerous for his son to be seen in public speaking to a man whom the chief priests and the officers of the Temple police were conspiring to arrest.[16]

One night, lying awake in bed in our quarters on the Mount of Olives overlooking the Kidron Valley, I just couldn't stand it any more. I got up, wrapped a bed sheet around myself to hide my nighttime nakedness, and slipped out to await Jesus and his disciples as they strolled through the garden. I hid behind a huge old olive tree—and I saw it all! The arrest, I mean. Suddenly there were soldiers and weapons and torches and that treacherous Judas, betraying his master with a kiss, and a sword-fight and then . . . silence . . . as Jesus gave himself over to the Temple police to be led away to the house of the High Priest.[17]

One of the policemen spotted me still hidden behind that tree. He shouted . . . ran toward me . . . and grabbed at me. I was terrified that I would be caught . . . and identified . . . and get my father in a whole lot of trouble! As the officer seized my bed sheet, I let it go . . . and ran . . . stark naked . . . into the night and back to my room.[18]

Next morning, I felt I had to tell my father what had happened. Instead of being furious with me, he was appalled at the apparent danger into which I had unknowingly thrust myself . . . and him! While my mother packed a trunk with basic travel necessities, my father designated one of his most trusted officers to get me out of Jerusalem and over to Caesarea as fast as he could. By late that very day, I was on a ship bound for

16. Luke 22:4.
17. Luke 22:47-54.
18. Mark 14:51-52.

Athens . . . and the beginning of my new life as a medical student.

I miss Palestine . . . and my parents . . . and the infrequent opportunities I used to have to spend time with the followers of Jesus. But I love Athens . . . and the university . . . and the classes I'm already taking . . . and the prospect of becoming a real doctor some day. Maybe I'll return to Palestine to practice . . . or maybe I'll get to travel all over the Empire. I already know that it will depend on where the God and Father that Jesus taught me about leads me.

But now that Jesus has been crucified, I wonder how long people will remember him and the marvelous things he did and all the wise lessons he taught. I've always kept a diary—ever since I was a little boy. I realize now that those scrolls are full of notes about the things Jesus said and did when he was in the Galilee. I don't think I wrote down the names of the people he helped and healed . . . but their stories are all there . . . the healings, the parables, the arguments with the Pharisees, the misunderstandings amongst the disciples, the sermons, the prayers . . . the unknown friends who helped Jesus and loved him and looked to him for courage and comfort and leadership and life everlasting.

Perhaps when I have my education and a flourishing medical practice and some free time, I'll write a book about Jesus . . . and the people around him . . . and the things he taught and the miracles he performed . . . and the way he embodied that love of the Father God he always talked about—a love that extends equally to everyone: rich or poor, strong or weak, young or old, saint or sinner—a love that embraces women and men and girls and boys in a hug that feels like the everlasting arms of the Creator.

I want to do what I can so that the world will never forget the most wonderful man who ever lived. For now, though, I have an anatomy class. Excuse me, please. I've got to go.

— XXI —

JACOB

BACKGROUND COMMENTARY

THROUGH ALL THE YEARS of my preaching ministry,
I stalwartly resisted the temptation to draw soliloquies
out of the Hebrew Scriptures. To "proclaim Christ crucified"[1] was ever my standard; and I thought it would be difficult—if not impossible—to overlay an Old Testament story
with a Gospel message. So I never tried . . .

With two exceptions. One year, when I undertook to
preach a series of sermons based on the Advent and Lenten
prophecies of Isaiah, I felt led to prepare my congregation with
a soliloquy in which I introduced the prophet himself and some
of his musings on the eventual fulfillment of his oracles.[2]

The other came to me at a time and place in my ministry I
shall not divulge out of respect for the family—and the memory—of a very dear elder who took his own life. On a beautiful
Saturday morning, he shot the top of his head off in his base-
ment while his wife washed the breakfast dishes in the kitchen
upstairs. This unforeseen tragedy shattered whatever pastoral
complacency I had wrapped around myself by then, and broke
the hearts of almost everyone in that close-knit congregation.

In the terrible aftermath of his suicide, even more terribly
tragic revelations began to surface. A private lifetime of alcohol
abuse and financial irresponsibility had virtually bankrupted
him and his family; an almost impenetrable web of deceit, de-

1. 1 Corinthians 1:23.
2. See CHAPTER I, "Here Am I: Send Me!"

nial, and desperation had made his public life a living hell; and so everyone who had known him and loved him and failed him felt bereft, bewildered, even betrayed.

After his funeral, I wondered how I could climb up into my safe and lofty pulpit the next Sunday and preach any message at all—let alone any word of comfort, or hope, or integrity. On a 3×5 index card in my "Sermon Ideas" box, I came upon an old note of someone else's sermon title I had once admired: "Wrestling with Remembered Wrongs." I have no idea whose title it was . . . or what his/her text might have been . . . but it immediately made me think of Jacob wrestling with an un-named and unknown assailant at the ford of the Jabbok stream.[3]

From that point, this monologue virtually wrote itself. I cannot claim any pride of authorship: I don't know from where within me the words and ideas and insights came. If ever the Holy Spirit took over and put me on autopilot, it was in the writing of this message.

I never tried that again! . . . and, in truth, it never happened quite like that again!

* * * * *

In seminary, one of my preaching professors told a story on himself and his attempt one Sunday to put the onus of his sermon preparation on the Holy Spirit. All through that week, he procrastinated or allowed himself to become preoccupied with other things than writing his weekly message. So, on Sunday morning, as he got up to preach, he prayed to this effect: "OK,

---

3. Genesis 32:22ff.

Holy Spirit: do your stuff!"

To which the Holy Spirit responded: "You're not pious, Paul; you're just lazy!"

I have never claimed to be pious. I hope that, as a preacher, I have never been lazy. When I reread this collection of what I consider to be the best of my life's work, I think that, on some Sundays at least, I was not!

* * * *

Wrestling with Remembered Wrongs

Then the man said,
"You shall no longer be called Jacob, but Israel,
for you have striven with God and with humans, and have prevailed."
So Jacob called the place Peniel, saying,
"For I have seen God face to face, and yet my life is preserved."
(GENESIS 32:28 AND 30)

Have you ever had a nightmare? . . . a dream so real it seizes you in a struggle-to-the-dawn all night long? . . . a vision so ephemeral it vanishes with the morn like the dew from the grass?

I've just spent a night like that: and the pounding of my heart . . . and the trembling in my arms . . . and the pain from my hip down my leg . . . are enough to make me think it was no nightmare at all.

My name is Jacob—or it was, until last night—and those are my tents and flocks and servants and family camped over there across the ford. I came back here to spend the night alone . . . to plot out my strategy for what could be the most im-

portant day of my life. I built a little fire to keep warm by . . . and
sat down in the sand to think . . . and had the strangest feeling
that I wasn't alone, after all.

I must have fallen asleep, because, from out of nowhere, a
hand seemed to seize me by the shoulder, spin me round in the
darkness, and wrestle me to the ground. As hard as I tried, I
could neither see my adversary nor wriggle out of his grasp.

At first, I figured it must be Laban, my father-in-law. He
was so angry when we finally left Haran to head for home . . .
and he has gone back on his word so many times . . . that it
would be just like him to sneak up on me in the darkness and
try to strangle or knife me.

You know, he made me work seven years for him—my own
uncle—for the privilege of marrying one of his daughters. Then
he tricked me into taking his eldest girl, Leah, as my bride, instead of my beloved Rachel . . . and then added insult to injury
by suggesting that I could work another seven years for Rachel's
hand.[4]

That was a long time ago, and I've prospered since—no
thanks to him! A few years ago, when I first wanted to go back
to my father's homeland, Laban magnanimously offered me my
"wages" for all those years of work. I agreed to take what he offered—just the spotted goats and black sheep from the flocks;
but before I could cull them out, he had his sons drive them all
away to other parts of the country . . . leaving me nothing. I fixed
him though: I bided my time, and carefully bred his sheep and
goats to my own purposes . . . until I ended up with huge flocks
of brindled goats and black sheep . . . and he was left with almost
nothing![5]

4. Genesis 29:15ff.
5. Genesis 30:25-43.

And how I hated him all those years . . . and resented his tricks and lies . . . and nursed my memories of every wrong he had ever done me . . . and enjoyed every thought of sweet revenge! As I wrestled against him in the darkness, I felt that I was wrestling against every dirty, deceitful, rotten wrong thing he had ever done to me . . . until I was too tired to hate him any more . . . too weary to resent him any longer . . . too spent to carry a grudge any farther—only to discover that it wasn't Laban I was wrestling at all.

It must be Esau, my twin brother, I decided . . . big-hearted, dull-witted, easy-going, impetuous Esau.

Now if anyone had reason to do me in in the dark of night, it was Esau. Even when we were boys, I always one-upped my brother, which made him angry, his being the older twin by a few minutes—like the time he was so hungry he swore an oath he would give me his birthright in exchange for a pot of soup and a hunk of bread.[6]

But he vowed he would kill me when I cheated him out of our father's deathbed blessing; so that's when I ran away to Haran to live with Uncle Laban.[7] It was so long ago. I was sure his anger would be cooled by now . . . but not forgotten.

Why should he forget his anger when I can't forget my shame? I knew I was running a tremendous risk, coming back like this. That's why I arranged my flocks and herds and servants into two groups, and sent half of them ahead in a long-drawn-out procession . . . with instructions to tell Esau that they were my present to him . . . figuring that I might be able to appease whatever anger he might still have. Together they must be worth more than whatever my father could have left!

6. Genesis 25:29-34.
7. Genesis 27:41-45.

But despite my shame and fear, when it seemed that Esau had surprised me in the dark, I couldn't bring myself to give in . . . to accept at his hands the punishment I so richly deserved . . . to cry out in remorse for the ways I had cheated him . . . to offer restitution of the blessing and the birthright I had tricked away from him.

As we struggled on in soul-shattering silence, I discovered to my horror that I had grown so accustomed to my guilt, so comfortable in my shame, that I was no longer really sorry. And in that instant, I realized that I was not wrestling with my brother, Esau, at all.

Was I wrestling with myself? . . . with all the remembered wrongs of Laban's shabby treatment of me, and all my shameful treachery against Esau? Was this where all my struggle and scheming and deceit and determination had got me? . . . writhing in fear and anguish by a burnt-out campfire in the dead of night? Would every night be like this from now on?

Haran was behind me, and Laban's years of cheating cruelty: could I ever forgive him for all he had done to me? Canaan lay ahead across the ford, and Esau was waiting somewhere in the wilderness: could he ever forgive me for all I had done to him?

Could I ever forgive myself? . . . I who harbored grudges . . . and plotted evil . . . and knew shame . . . but felt no remorse . . . no pity . . . no emotion save fear? Could God ever forgive me . . . when I was so stiff-necked . . . so proud . . . so crafty . . . so determined to make it on my own?

On and on I struggled through the night, remembering every wrong I had ever done . . . every wrong that had ever been done to me—regretting, resentful, wretched—but never re-morseful. Like a madman, I was determined to prevail, deter-mined to outlast my assailant—whoever—whatever—he might be.

As the darkness dragged on and utter weariness threatened to overwhelm me, I began to remember another night . . . an-other struggle of the soul . . . another apparition. It had all hap-pened when I first ran away from home so many years before: I had stopped to rest at Bethel, and in my sleep had seen a ladder stretching to heaven from the ground, and angels of God going up and down it. The Lord God had been standing beside the ladder and had spoken to me of His promises to my fathers and to me—that our family should become numerous, and be blessed with land and prosperity. Well, that much had already begun to come true![8]

But God had promised something more, I remembered—something I had never thought about in all the years since. "I will be with you," God had said, " and I will protect you wher-ever you go, and will bring you back to this land; for I will not leave you until I have done all that I have promised."[9]

Was that what I was struggling against?—the lingering un-recognized presence of God in my life?—the growing but-as-yet-unadmitted realization that it was not my scheming and struggling that had brought me my success but rather God's goodness and providence?

Had I deceived my father, cheated my brother, endured my uncle, married my wives, fathered my children, built my fortune, plotted my return, nursed my resentment, hidden my shame, and gloried in my self-sufficiency, all in vain?

8. Genesis 28:10ff.
9. Genesis 28:15.

Would my family be just as numerous today, my wealth just as great, my future just as secure—or even more so?—had I simply trusted in God's promises, and humbly followed the unfolding of God's providence? Surely not!!! Surely not!!!

As if to silence the desperate rebellion of my soul, my assailant struck my thigh a superhuman blow. The pain was excruciating; the hip felt dislocated; the fight went out of me at last. Then, softly and tenderly, in a voice I recognized at once, almost by way of explanation and apology, my no-longer-unknown assailant said, "Let me go, for day is breaking."

In the dark of night, and in the deeper darkness of my rebellious soul, I understood that I had seen—and been struggling with—God . . . face to face . . . and yet, my life had been spared! Guilt . . . and remorse . . . and anger at my own stupidity . . . and desperation that God should disappear into the dawn and leave me like this . . . welled up into one last outburst of all the strength I had left—a cry for blessing, for benediction, for forgiveness, for cleansing, for hope, for peace.

The struggle was over . . . and God had won. The ache in my hip lingered . . . but the ache in my soul was gone—and with it, my disrespect of my father . . . my hatred of my uncle . . . my fear of my brother . . . my mistrust of my wives . . . my remorselessness of heart . . . my self-sufficiency of spirit.

I could forgive—for I was forgiven. I could forget—for I was cleansed. I could face the future—for I was at peace. How simple it all seems now! . . . but how much I had put myself through to find out! God does love me . . . God does care about me . . . God does watch over me . . . in spite of all I have done to foil God's promises and to frustrate God's providence.

Before He left me—and, strange as it may seem, I don't feel that He has left me at all—though I can no longer see or feel Him the way I did while we were struggling—before He left me, God gave me a new name: "Israel."

"Israel"—it means, I'm ashamed to say, something like "God strove" or "God struggled" to win me.

I wonder whether that shouldn't be every believer's name? For surely each of us struggles with God . . . and God surely struggles to win each one of us. He loves us all: yet, each of us, in our own way, denies that love . . . and determines to do things the way we like. Not everyone turns into a scheming, cheating rascal like me, but we all find our own ways of going wrong . . . and doing wrong . . . and being wrong . . . and wrestling with wrong . . . until God steps in to make things right. We're all too selfish to forgive . . . to stubborn to be forgiven . . . too smart to forgive ourselves . . . until God pins us down somewhere and pains us into submission somehow and puts us right with one another . . . and with Him . . . and with ourselves.

My father is dead . . . my uncle left behind . . . my brother— well, who knows what my brother will do when we meet later this morning! But I know what I shall do. I shall ask for his forgiveness . . . restore what I have cheated from him . . . work for our reconciliation . . . and trust God to take care of the rest.

Has God had to struggle for you the way He strove for me? Have you let Him forgive you the way He has forgiven me?

If *not*—and even more, if *so*—what are you going to do about it?

Easton, Matthew George. *Easton's Bible Dictionary*. Oak Harbor: Logos, 1997.

Frank, Harry Thomas, ed. *Hammond's Atlas of the Bible Lands*. Revised ed. Maplewood: Hammond, 1997.

Keck, Leander E., senior editor. *The New Interpreter's Bible*. 12 vols. Nashville: Abingdon Press, 1994-2003.

Peterson, Eugene H. *The Message: The Bible in Contemporary Language*. Colorado Springs: NavPress, 2002.

The Presbyterian Hymnal: Hymns, Psalms and Spiritual Songs. Louisville: Westminster/John Knox Press, 1990.

ORN AND RAISED IN Windsor, Ontario, Canada, Bill studied
philosophy at the University of Toronto and theology at Knox
College, Toronto, and Princeton Theological Seminary. Early
in his ministry in the (then) United Presbyterian Church (USA), he
served as an assistant minister at the Fifth Avenue Presbyterian
Church in mid-town Manhattan and as the senior pastor of the
Wyoming Presbyterian Church in Millburn–Short Hills, New Jersey.

In 1973, he was called to the Church of St. Andrew and St. Paul
in Montreal, Quebec—the "cathedral church of Canadian Presbyterians." As part of his ministry there, he was appointed chaplain to the
Black Watch (Royal Highland Regiment) of Canada and its Colonel-
in-Chief, Her Majesty Queen Elizabeth the Queen Mother, whom
he served with distinction for ten years and then remained in contact
for the rest of Her Majesty's long life.

After a decade of providing significant, and often dangerous,
leadership to the English-speaking minority in Quebec during that
province's first wave of nationalism and separatist fervor, Bill was
called to be the General Secretary and Chief Executive Officer of the
Canadian Bible Society. In the six-and-a-half years of his Bible Society
ministry, he traveled extensively in the Bible cause, visiting some 30
countries on five continents, many of them "third-world" destinations
behind the "Iron Curtain" and in Latin America. Due to severe ill-
nesses both he and his wife, Ann, contracted during their last visit to
four countries in the South American Andes, the Russells retired in

1988 to their beloved lakehouse just outside Rondeau Provincial Park on the north shore of Lake Erie in southwestern Ontario.

After a year's convalescence, during which Bill trained to become accredited for intentional interim ministry by the Interim Network out of Baltimore, Maryland, he was called unexpectedly to Deerfield, Illinois, a "north shore" suburb of Chicago for a ten-year senior pastorate, after which he moved to Royal Oak, Michigan, to a similar ministry much nearer his aging parents back in Windsor. Plagued by ill-health again, Bill took early retirement at the end of 2001, after two major surgeries and the loss of his mother to Alzheimer's. The heartbreaking stress of the sudden and unexpected death of his wife, Ann, a few months later, and then of his father a few months after that, brought to an unfortunate and unfulfilled close his 40 years of active ministry.

Untimely retirement brought unexpected recovery, however, and in the winter of 2003-4, Bill went to Destin, Florida for a few months, met, fell in love with, and courted the former Sharon (Sherri) Nelson Fuss. They were married at Bill's Canadian lakehouse on July 4, 2004; now they spend half the year at Bill's mountain home in Somerset, Kentucky, and the remainder at Sherri's long-time home in Destin's Kelly Plantation.

Health and strength restored, Bill has become a "rent-a-rev" (his e-mail domain name), and makes himself available for supply and interim preaching, weddings, funerals, and pastoral counseling in south central Kentucky and Florida's Emerald Coast. His collection of Scripture-based soliloquies and monologues keep him much in demand as a guest preacher in churches large and small.

INTERESTED READERS MAY E-MAIL
DR. RUSSELL PERSONALLY AT
soliloquies@rentarev.us.